THE LION'S MARKET

God's Currency

by

DOUGLAS KENT

THE LION'S MARKET: God's Currency

©2018 Douglas Kent

First printing September 2018

Published by Douglas Kent, Wewahitchka, FL ISBN-13: 978-0692191163 (Lion's Market, The) ISBN-10: 069219116X

Cover Artwork by: Latasha Brown

All rights reserved. No part of the publication may be reproduced, stored in a retrieval system or transmitted in any format by any means – electronic, mechanical, photocopy, recording, or any other – except for brief quotation in printed reviews, with the proper permission of the publisher.

CONTENTS

THE LION'S MARKET 1
THE CURRENCY 5
MARKETPLACE CHRISTIANITY 7
LION'S MARKET STRATEGY 13
VOLUNTEERS 17
INTERDEPENDENT VS INDEPENDENT 19
MARKET FORCES 21
GIVING WITH VOLUNTEERS 27
THE ETERNAL ECONOMY 31
DEMAND 39
THE TREASURY 43
THE SEVEN MOUNTAINS 47
GIVE ME MY MOUNTAIN 51
STEWARDSHIP 55
WANTS 61
PLACE OF THE CHURCH 63
YEAR OF JUBILEE 67
CONNECTIONS AND RELATIONSHIPS 71
UNITY 77
KINGDOM LABOR 85
KINGDOM WELFARE 91
MAMMON 95

INTRODUCTION

In 2009 I first heard the term "The Lion's Market". I had no idea what it meant but I did know that it sparked something inside of me. The Holy Spirit had planted a 'seed' my heart, but I had no idea that it's revelation would take years to unfold.

I asked the Holy Spirit to give me some understanding about it for months and then finally one morning I woke up to the beginning of the Lion's Market revelation. The Lord began to unveil His 'economic model' that was the 'Lion's Market'. It was far superior to anything the world had or could ever produce.

Since 2009 I have been compiling the revelation and notes given by the Holy Spirit and finally felt it was time to organize them into this book. And I am sure that additional revelation will continue to manifest, and I know that I am not the only one who will be receiving it.

THE ESSENCE

The Lion's market is not just a different version of a financial system, it operates at a much higher level, a heavenly one. It is not just about the production of material wealth it is about Christians being led by the Holy Spirit in every aspect of their lives and the resulting abundance of LIFE that changes communities and nations.

God has placed us precisely and gifted us perfectly in order to be leaders and influencers in our businesses and communities. The principles of Godly living as made plain throughout the Holy Scriptures are the foundation to the Lion's Market. It's NOT RELIGION in the marketplace, it is TRUTH and INTEGRITY which align us with God's purposes resulting in abundance and TRANSFORMATION in our communities, nations and globally!

1
THE LION'S MARKET

The term "Lion's Market," was released in a prophetic word in 2009 at a service at the Christian International ministry headquarters in Santa Rosa Beach, FL. The prophet speaking at the time said that we would go to a "Lion's Market". Nothing more was explained but it was a seed that was planted in my heart.

I dwelt on it and asked God what it meant. I was thinking that night that it was probably similar to today's stock market system and would arise out it. I know we have the Bear market and the Bull Market, but I kept seeking the Holy Spirit on revelation about how the Lion's Market would work?

Four months later I was surprised one morning when the Holy Spirit provided me spiritual insight into the workings of it. He instructed me that the Lion's Market is an everlasting market and that portions of it already existed. It was explained as a perpetual market that is not cyclical. God was revealing the Lion's Market and unveiling a biblical truth. It has always been around us but we did not discern or understand it.

I would say "it is like many of the unveilings of biblical truths" that have been released by the Holy Spirit throughout the ages. Examples are; the just shall live by faith, sanctification by grace, holiness, and baptism of the Holy Ghost. Each had to be unveiled and had to be preached for believers to walk and grasp God's provisions in their day. And now it's time for the Lion's Market.

THE ETERNAL MARKET

On April 7, 2014, I heard the Lord say, "It is the season and now is the time for the Lion's Market to arise. It will no longer be the Bull or Bear Market as the world sees it, but it will become the Lion's Market in this third and final reformation.

The Bull and Bear Market is cyclical and results in financial failure but I, the Lord, has called for the true Market of the Lion. I say My Currency is everlasting and my economic policy is for this age and the one eternal." The Lord continued, "What you learn of my economic Lion's Market here and now will not change, for my Kingdom's exchange rate and currency is the same throughout my Kingdom territories. My currency is **FAITH**. Goods and products that are everlasting in this life and one to come and will remain for eternity are bought through this Currency of Faith. The Redeemed will use this currency to purchase hope, love, healing, and power. This faith can close the mouths of lions, conquer fear, subdue kingdoms, save households, raise the dead and bring everlasting life to the spiritually dead."

This passage from Revelation chapter three indicates the Lord's desire for His disciples to operate above the world system of buying and selling material and temporary goods:

"*I counsel you to buy from Me gold refined in the fire, that you may be rich; and white garments, that you may be clothed, that the shame of your nakedness may not be revealed; and anoint your eyes with eye salve, that you may see.*" Revelation 3:17-19

The Lion's Market is for us to go into all the world bringing Life and Light. The principles mentioned in this writing are not new, but I hope will provide insight into a spiritual truth that needs to take root in the Church. It is time for it (us) to rise up, occupy and possess. It is TRUTH that when preached and acted upon will bring deliverance to the land and freedom to people in bondage. Our co-dependency with this world system will be dissolved and the illusions of the enemy will be dissipated. It is a truth for a self-sustaining Church in times of abundance and blessing, but also times of tribulation.

TODAY, TOMORROW AND FOREVER

The Lion's Market is at work today and the eternal laws that govern its operation are unwavering. No matter what is going on in the world, good times or bad times the Lion's Market is functioning. And not only in this present age but it will also be working in the New Kingdom and in the days of the new heaven and new earth!

We are seeing but not perceiving even though everyone is looking. It is as Jesus described when he said to the Pharisees "You see but you are blind."

"But when He was alone, those around Him with the twelve asked Him about the parable. [11] And He said to them, "To you it has been given to know the mystery of the kingdom of God; but to those who are outside, all things come in parables, [12] so that ' Seeing they may see and not perceive, And hearing they may hear and not understand; Lest they should turn And their sins be forgiven them.'" Matthew 4:10

I would like to say that we can see now because it is time for the unveiling. I am not an Economist, but the Holy Spirit is and God's revelation is for this season. So, from the written truth (Logos) the following Rhema word is released and flows to an eternal people, an eternal Church for an eternal 'economic market'.

The insight you should receive is that God has always had an eternal economic system to finance his work. We see it over and over again where people are led by the Holy Spirit to "work" in halfway houses, schools, hospitals, churches, youth, and other life-changing organizations. Some of the basic principles like understanding the call, volunteerism, giving, stewardship is part of the Lion's Market strategies with a foundation of freedom I call Entrepreneurism.

2
THE CURRENCY
The Lion's Market Currency is not kept in a bank

Currency is any standardized form of exchange. It has a set value and is used commonly to purchase goods and services within a society, geographic area or even globally. It is sometimes surprising to learn that God's Kingdom also has a currency.

"Ho, everyone that thirsts, come you to the waters, and he that has no money; come you, buy and eat; yea come, buy wine and milk without money and without price" Is 55:1
"I counsel you to buy from me (The Lord Jesus) gold refined in the fire, so you can become rich, and white clothes to wear, so you can cover your shameful nakedness. and salve to put on your eyes, so you can see." Rev 3:18

The Lord is counselling His people to 'buy' from Him, not physical goods or services, but items that have value not only for today but more importantly, for eternity. What could we possibly possess that can be used as currency for these eternal 'items'? What could anyone possibly have that is of any value to the King of Kings and Lord of Lords, the God of all creation? Faith.

FAITH

We are all familiar with Romans 10:17, "Faith comes by hearing, and hearing by the Word (Rhema and Logos) of God." And we understand that hearing is not the end of it, but that we must also put it into practice. God is constantly speaking to us in many ways. As we become more sensitive to His voice and quicker to respond to His direction (with a joyful heart!) our faith grows, and our heavenly 'account' increases.

This Faith is more than just believing that God exists. In James 2:19 we see that even demons believe He (God) exists, and they tremble. So again, this Faith is more than just belief, it's the fruit of a love relationship that is pure and deep between the Lord God and us His children. It's the fruit of a relationship that is bringing about a transformation of our soul and mind and their divine alignment with the Holy Spirit.

This Faith, this eternal 'currency' allows the very power of God to flow into and through our lives. This currency is what allows us to 'purchase' from God, His gold, food, drink, clothing and eye salve. True Kingdom provision that will enable you to live the Abundant Life. You will become a manifestation of the promise found in Hebrews 11:6 'that God is a rewarder of those who diligently seek Him'. As you live every part of your life on the foundation of this Faith, this Kingdom currency, you will find that God's provision will flow increasingly and abundantly into and through you.

3
MARKETPLACE CHRISTIANITY
Birthing Entrepreneurs for the Lion's Market

In 2009 I heard the Lord say, *"This is the time for the birthing of entrepreneurs in the Lion's Market"*

Lion's Market = Kingdom Market

"Be diligent to present yourself approved to God, a worker who does not need to be ashamed, rightly dividing the word of truth." 2 Timothy 2:15

I picked up a business card at a craft fair in Tallahassee, Florida. It was from Ronald Mozee, a very skilled and creative entrepreneur. This man of God truly demonstrated the Kingdom of God in his work. He had great talent using his creative art skills to make ornate ink pens and shadow boxes using antlers, horns and rare woods. Every item he crafts shares the touch of the Master's hand and the love of God. Ronald is a living demonstration of God in his sphere of influence in the business mountain. He found his niche, his destiny, and that not only makes him happy, but it fulfills God's will for his life.

IT'S ABOUT ALL OF US

We need to stop thinking that secular work and talent is in some way ungodly. A plumber, carpenter, welder, babysitter etc. can be the finger of God while at their work. God's intent has always been to use His church body to do His work and provide the 'light' of His mercy and grace in all parts of this dark world. I believe that it's time for the

Kingdom citizens, born-again Christians to truly possess their land. God's principals, strategies, and favor allow His people to receive the wealth of the world.

When the children of Israel left Egypt as recorded in the Book of Exodus, they were given gifts and presents by the Egyptians. We read in Proverbs 13:22, *"But the wealth of the sinner is stored up for the righteous."* When a child of God is walking (living) in His will, in their destiny, God will provide His divine favor. You must be a person of integrity, honesty and with the willingness to do what is right in God's sight. You must be humble but with the strength and boldness of a lion's heart.

My Pastor, Tom Hamon, says that when you are born again, like in John chapter 3, you become a new creation and your DNA changes from Deoxyribonucleic Acid to 'Divine Natural Attributes'. As a medical biologist, I call it a mutation to the Divine. We become a new creature and a new species that is alive in the spirit. We can enter it, see it, hear it and in so doing possess the Kingdom of God.

"And the stone that struck the image became a great mountain and filled the whole earth." Daniel 2:34

God will finally prevail when Jesus puts everything under his feet. But until Jesus comes back, we are His agents to establish His Kingdom in the places we occupy. Now we can see and understand the revelation and teaching of Lance Wallnau and the 7 Cultural Mountains or Spheres. The mandate for ALL of God's people is to live lives overflowing with Love and Truth and Power.

All in the body of Christ are called to be influencers in their Mountain; Religion, Education, Financial, Entertainment, Media, Family, and Business. As the church takes its rightful place, we will be able to bless the nations as Joseph did in Egypt. This was a nation that was completely ungodly but was blessed by a man of God. Joseph had a vision and divine wisdom that saved a nation and the surrounding region.

MY EXAMPLE

I can use myself as an example as a Healthcare Entrepreneur. I was coming to work one morning after several years of being a Health Officer for a small County in Northwest Florida. It was a position God appointed me to (a good story in itself, that I share later).

The Lord spoke to me as I was going to work on a Monday, telling me to put in a digital X-Ray machine for the County. At the time, the local hospital was defunct and closed and doctors had no access to a local X-Ray in the whole County. Everyone had to make an hour's drive to reach the closest ER or a diagnostic imaging facility. I know it's hard to image in the 21st Century, that an entire county in Florida would not have its own X-Ray capability.

Well, as I approached the top of a bridge going to work that morning the Lord told me that He wanted me to put in digital X- Ray for the County. My first response was, "Lord I don't know anything about digital X-Ray". I know some of you are skeptical about hearing God's voice but that is normal for me. Matter of fact, every born-again Christian has had to hear God's 'voice' at least once! You got saved, didn't you?

Over the course of my many years walking with the Lord, I have found that when God gives a command, most of the time, He includes very few details.

When I expressed my ignorance about what God wanted to be done, I sensed that He was not concerned. So, as I was driving I started thinking about where I could even put the unit in my building since we did not have any available space.

I decided to move the Medical Library and close off a hallway and thought to myself, "that would work." Next, I went to the office and researched what needed to take place to implement the plan. I found out through the internet it would cost between $150,000 and $175,000 dollars for the equipment. Plus, I was going to need the local County worker maintenance Department to change the room, add lead lining to the walls and upgrade the electrical.

We had county supervisors' meetings every Monday morning and I had shared with my staff that I felt that we needed to put digital X-ray in for the County (I did not say that God had said so!). By this time my supervisors had been a part of many extraordinary projects and knew that If I said it, it was possible. One of them asked the cost and I informed them of the price tag and then they asked how much money I had for the project. I said that I had zero dollars, but it will come.

That was a Monday. On Wednesday the small town has a paper that comes out once a week. Somehow without my guidance, a statement was noted on the front page, "Health Department needs equipment." I did not call the paper, it just showed up on the front page.

Thursday Morning a mother and daughter showed up at my office wanting to speak with me. Since I'm also the complaint department I assumed they had an issue, so I told the front desk to bring them on back. When they sat down we had a short conversation and then the daughter informed me that her mother read in the paper that the Health Department needed equipment. I informed her that was correct, and she then said that her mother wanted to give a donation.

I told them that I'm a State agency and I'm not sure if we can accept donations from the general public. I found out that it was okay and then asked them how much they wanted to give.

She then said that she wanted to write me a check for $100,000. I turned my chair to my window and said to God, 'You do want this digital X-ray.' Graciously I accepted the offer and the next day, Friday, I enlarged my vision! Since God was truly in it I grew the budget to $250,000 and added a movable table, real-time event and read through system read by a group from Sacred Heart Medical in 30 min or less.

So, God wanted it done right, not halfway and it would be the best quality service available. When I got to work the next Monday, I got a call from the county attorney who asked, 'Doug do you know the defunct hospital?' I said, 'Yes, of course', and he said he just got together with the Judge and he ruled that my X- ray project fit the endowment objectives that were set up for that hospital.

He said that the judge has ruled the remaining endowment money could be used for the X-ray. I had not called him or advised him of the project God had birthed in me. To this date, I do not know how he found out anything about the project other than that it was God using His people to make his desires manifest.

The lawyer said the money left was $150,000! Wow is God good! God revealed to me thru this project and to several others the He loves everyone.

"While we were yet sinners Christ died for us." Romans 5:8

God's mercy, grace, and love are provided for all mankind. He uses His servants as His hands in the earth. Within seven days God had provided all the funding for this desperately needed and compassionate project which would serve the health care needs of an entire community. God provided the vision, provision, talent and technical people throughout the project to ensure its success.

God is birthing Lion's Market Entrepreneurs who are people with vision and:

1: A call to serve
2: Resources
3: Talents
4: Goals
5: Values
6: Opportunities

They recognize the Lion's Share which is that portion of market resources that are available to leverage and create a competitive advantage in the marketplace.

The world will not (cannot) see the spiritual resources available for the vision or call. Resources like time, personnel and money will not appear to be abundant but through spiritual eyes, you will by faith see the starting point. Strategies will be given by the Spirit of God that will position your organization and leaders for precise tactical moves. Proper executions can then occur in the marketplace for Godly programs to succeed, bringing glory to God and blessings to a community. Lion's Market strategies delivered by the Holy Ghost provide for the needs of an organization.

Christian Entrepreneurs in the Lion's Market demonstrate this scripture:

"For in Him we live and move and have our being, as also some of your own poets have said, 'For we are also His offspring." Acts 17:28

4
LION'S MARKET STRATEGY
The Revelation of 'The Lion's Share'

The Lion's Share is that portion of market resources that we as Christian Entrepreneurs are afforded and that can be used as leverage for a competitive advantage. Resources like time, personnel and money may not appear to be abundant, but, through spiritual eyes, you will by faith be able to see a starting point and steps that follow.

Divine strategies given by the Spirit of God will position your organization and leaders for tactical moves so that proper executions can be made resulting in Godly programs increasing in a community. Lion's Market strategies when delivered by the Holy Ghost provide not necessarily what the organization wants but **exactly** what it needs.

The key to each Godly work, like other successful organizations, will be developed by a unique Lion's market strategy. Organizations and leaders will begin to act out their faith and God will attract investors for their work. Organizations will demonstrate Godly confidence to the people that are offering the investments and one of their 'returns' on their investment will be victory over demonic influence.

GOD MAKES THE IMPOSSIBLE POSSIBLE

A Lion's Market strategy is prayed over and when implemented will differentiate your work from the world's. To many, your ideas might seem impossible or even unnecessary but with time they will be seen as being desperately needed or so creative that no one else could have thought them up.

In the Lion's Market, customers are valued for their souls rather than what they have to give. The realization of God's plan for their life is the essential goal, profitability is secondary. Wealth creation is the paramount management goal in the world market however in the Lion's Market the work of FAITH *"which is an assurance of things hoped for and surety of things not seen"* (Heb 11:1) is the Lion's Share that brings eternal increase.

Lion's Market Strategies incorporate these core fundamentals which enable the Lion's Share:

- Your brand or product development is completely God-inspired, and the marketplace perceives it by Spirit.
- You cannot copy other works or organizations, it must be by faith and each will be unique.
- Your service isn't your final product or marker of success, it is your total commitment to the work even (or especially) when service does not look fruitful.

You cannot change the core call so be faithful to the direction the Holy Spirit provides and you will be a partaker in the Lion's Share!

MY CALL

After 17 years as an Environmentalist and now as Health Administrator over two different Counties, I need to say to people you must push through on your destiny or calling. After going back to college to receive my Public Health Masters, my drive was to become a Health Officer over a County or Health District.

My goal I felt was that God is the provider for my life, and that I was to be the best at whatever position I was working. This would be a testimony to those over me and the ones I worked with. I would demonstrate that I would make a great executive.

It so happened, that after several years the doctor who was the Director where I worked decided to leave and he came into my office and said, "Doug, I think you would make an excellent health office over this county and I will recommend you."

I was ecstatic, and the State made me the Acting Director, one of the first non-doctors in the State. However, after several days the District Tallahassee Doctor came into my office and informed that she was not recommending me and if she gets another phone call, email or mail from people advocating for me she was going to fire me.

At that point the Spirit of the Lord raised up in me and I said to her that I had worked for 7 Directors and if there is an eighth she missed the chance to have the best director the County has ever had. Not bragging but knowing the heart of God and my willingness to hear and be led by his Spirit.

Hearing the voice of God in secular jobs is critically important to bring the Kingdom of God into the Seven Mountains of influence over whatever position you are working. I went home and said to my wife, if God wants me to have the job He will have to give it to me because the District Doctor said she was not going to recommend me.

Several weeks later that same Doctor came into my office and told me that she had changed her mind and would recommend me. I went home that night and said to my wife that God had given me the job.

God does determine leadership and sets conditions up for us to fight our battles and press toward His high mark for our lives. God gave me provision to go from 12 people to 87 and from a $750,000 budget to $4.5M budget. Also, 90% of the community was now taking advantage of the great medical care and public health resources and using the

facility. My goal was 100% access and zero disparities before I moved onto the next pathway God had approved.
I can truthfully say 100% access was achieved for the community. Regardless of ability to pay you could be seen for the following services that where available that previously had not been. We now offered women's health, mental health, primary care, after- hour care, dental, orthopedic, digital x-ray etc.

Doing good things for great people was my goal (God's goal). A true example of working in the Lion's Market when we say YES to His Word, Will and Way.

5
VOLUNTEERS
Selfless Servants Serving

*"The LORD shall send the rod of Your strength out of Zion. Rule in the midst of Your enemies! Your people **shall be volunteers** in the day of Your power; In the beauties of holiness, from the womb of the morning, You have the dew of Your youth. The LORD has sworn And will not relent, "You are a priest forever according to the order of Melchizedek." Psalms 110:2-4*

We see God's plan coming together and this scripture being fulfilled with more and more Christian volunteers taking action. Jesus' servants will be people who volunteer for His work. In these last days, God's volunteer army will be a key component in His plan in ushering in His Kingdom.

All of God's people should have hearts to build and serve. Against all odds volunteers start ministries and by faith, they thrive.
Volunteerism for the 3rd and final reformation's Saints Movement is starting to take place in this last age of grace.

Faith without works (deeds/action) is dead, so faith-motivated works unlock market forces for the righteous, and belief unlocks God's provision for them to have a right to receive. The scripture says that "Abraham believed God and it was accounted to him for righteousness" (Gen 15:6)

Ezra going back to Jerusalem depended on volunteers to rebuild the temple of God.

"I issue a decree that all those of the people of Israel and the priests and Levites in my realm, who volunteer to go up to Jerusalem, may go with you." Ezra 7:13

Even the pagan king, Artaxerxes, recognized the giving spirit that resides in a servant of God and made way for the exiled Israelites to return to their homeland and begin its restoration.

TODAY'S VOLUNTEERS

Today, people volunteer to start and serve in ministries that feed, clothe and support thousands in need. Some of these ministries include Feed the Children, Mercy Ministry and Covenant House in Kinard, FL, (which I support). The heart and compassion of the Lord will be evident in His volunteers as they serve with joy.

The Lord God is saying, "Today is the time to fully start the release of the Lion's Market principles to the Church."

While the principle of Volunteering seems simple, it is POWERFUL and will be one of the major forces that allow the Church to 'invade' and take dominion of all 7 mountains of cultural influence.

Be it in business, education, government, media, entertainment etc. who can reject free donated skills, abilities or talents? Even the world understands the value in quality volunteers -and the light of the Kingdom will just keep spreading and spreading!

6

INTERDEPENDENT vs INDEPENDENT
A three-braided cord is not easily broken

In the World Market, the focus is placed on being Independent because 'it's all about me'. Selfishness is accepted to a point where the people who gain and hoard wealth (with no regard for others) are idolized. Their life is filled with worldly desires, but they are empty vessels on the inside, always seeking for more and never satisfied.

*"For there are many, of whom I have often told you, and now tell you even with tears, who live as enemies of the cross of Christ [rejecting and opposing His way of salvation], whose fate is destruction, **whose god is their belly** [their worldly appetite, their sensuality, their vanity], and whose glory is in their shame—who focus their mind on earthly and temporal things."* Philippians 3:18,19 (Amplified Version)

Those who participate in the World Market are slaves to their soul's; appetites, desires and, thirsts. They are 'lovers of self' and always searching for more, but never coming to the saving knowledge of Christ. Fleeting moments of happiness is all that a person with no settlement of peace in their heart can hope for because their god is them self. The Western culture exalts independence, but apart from the Lord it only leads to enslavement to darkness.

To the contrary, in the Lion's Market, the goal is true interdependence. It requires us to realize our need to work with each other thus bringing an excitement to living with all our vulnerability and insecurity. Interdependence adds value to all who are involved and ensures an improved result due to the benefits of synergy.

In the Lion's Market, the value of work produced has a direct relationship to the interdependence involved in the process. The products and/or services will be of higher quality both materially and spiritually. In the World Market where Independence is exalted products and/or services will be substandard (in comparison) and without spiritual merit.

7
MARKET FORCES

Hunger, Compassion, Grace and Love are a few of the forces that will trigger market shifts in value in the Lion's Market. It was very interesting when God shared with me that 'Hunger' was a huge force that not only moves the World Market but also the Lion's Market. However, in the Lion's Market, Hunger is different, it is the hunger for righteousness and peace.

"Blessed are those who hunger and thirst after righteousness, for they will be filled." Matthew 5:6

The Lion's Market gives value to a person who has right-standing with God. Their hunger is only satisfied by the Lord, "taste and see the Lord is Good". The Word is bread to the soul and gives life to all that find it. The word of God is bread and life, but it has no value in the World Market.

A body of believers driven by hunger to volunteer can truly change the world and manifest *"Thy will be done on earth as it is in heaven"* from the Lord's Prayer. Think of the number of individuals throughout history who have changed the world by their hunger to obey God.

Like Abraham, David, Martin Luther, George Washington, Martin Luther King Jr. *"We live not by bread alone but every word that proceeds out of the mouth of God."* Deuteronomy 8:2-3

Ministries are for the hopeless and the forgotten. Every ministry comes from an assignment and a call by God to make a difference. Again, and again ministers are asked, Acts 4:7 *"...By what power or*

by what name have you done this?" **Each time the name of Jesus Christ is invoked, the infinite power and force of Grace is unveiled. This force can shift individuals, cities and nations with an economic impact that is 'half the cost' of what the world requires and always with a MUCH better social outcome.**

THE FORCE OF FAITH

We know that Faith is the currency of the Kingdom, so then what are the forces and influences that work in the Kingdom. THESE FORCES occur and overcome natural forces using God's Laws.

We can recognize this as the 'flip' occurs in events, or as the Facts are overridden by The Truth. Christian International Bishop, Bill Hamon, says in his writings that a doctor deals in facts but that we as Christians deal in Truth. As we continually see, facts can change, new information can come to light and what everyone thought was correct is no longer the case. TRUTH on the other hand is eternal and never-changing.

Everyone is familiar with John 14:6 *"Jesus answered, 'I am the way and the truth and the life. No one comes to the Father except through me.'"* And in Paul's Epistle to the Galatians in chapter 5 and verses 22 and 23 we are told, *"But the fruit of the Spirit is love, joy, peace, forbearance, kindness, goodness, faithfulness, gentleness and self-control. Against such things* **there is no law.**" The Truth is a Person! The actions and behavior of a believer and follower of Jesus Christ will translate into thriving in the Lion's Market.

We can consider the influences from faith and how it 'shifts the atmosphere' by looking at a magnet. It has an invisible field that surrounds it which can influence susceptible metals when close by. A magnet can be used to 'overcome' the laws of nature in certain situations. If you hold a paper clip below a magnet it overcomes the law of gravity as it is drawn up to the magnet. The magnetic force that is not seen influences and counters the law of gravity.

In the Lion's Market, the force of faith can 'trump' facts that are defined by natural laws. Faith when present can change the direction of events just like a magnet can a resting paper clip. In the Gospel of Matthew, it says, 'if you have faith the size of a mustard seed and you say unto this mountain be the removed and it will be'. Now that is a FORCE!

In the book of Daniel in Chapter 3 we see the rock that is cut out but not with human hands. It smashes the supreme kingdoms of man and then becomes a huge Mountain that fills the whole earth. That mountain is the Kingdom of God in which the Lion's Market exists.

It is not going to change when Jesus comes back. No! It will always be present. There is one Church and One Kingdom and one Lion's Market. Faith 'shifts' the atmosphere. It opens the physical realm to God's Kingdom and the gifts of the Spirit are manifested. The Book of Jude says to 'Build up your most holy faith praying in the Holy Ghost.' So, to change atmosphere start praying in the Holy Ghost.

THE FORCE OF BELIEF

The next Lion's Market force is Belief. Belief is a Lion's Market mover, shifter and influencer.

"And without faith it is impossible to please God, because anyone who comes to Him must believe that He exists and that He rewards those who earnestly seek Him." Hebrews 11:6

We can see the Spirit-led market influencer can and will overcome even natural laws. If we can move mountains how hard is it to speed deals or find favor in negotiations or even the courtroom? In the World Market the influencers such as greed, deception, pride and sexual sin only serve to feed man's ego and lust which results in the spread of the kingdom of darkness.

We see it every day with the wanton excesses of the wealthy and their continual lust for more riches and power. The Bible teaches us that there is no fullness apart from the Lord, and without Him we will be always trying to fill our empty souls.

JOSEPH AND DANIEL

"Then the Lord answered me and said: "Write the vision and make it plain on tablets, that he may run who reads it. For the vision is yet for an appointed time; But at the end it will speak, and it will not lie. Though it tarries, wait for it; Because it will surely come, It will not tarry. "Behold the proud, His soul is not upright in him; But the just shall live by his faith." Habakkuk 2:2-4

In the scripture above we see that the vision is received (by one with faith) and then there is an appointment of a believing leader or leaders, men or women of God to carry out the task. It is completely voluntary, but one feels compelled to please the heart of God. His heart becomes our heart to please our King.

The heart of God is to provide for and through his people. Throughout the Bible we see God choose leaders and people to accomplish His will. You can look at Joseph, who saved a nation because he saw God's hand in his final position as second ruler over Egypt. He said that God prepared him for "such a time as this" Gen 45:4 "...for God sent me before you to preserve you."

Joseph's relationship to the living God throughout his trials was one that preserved (and matured) his character through the tests. He became attuned to hearing God's voice and interpreting dreams. He could discern the time and seasons. He saved a nation and his people in time of a seven-year famine.

God will rise up in these last ages men who will have an assignment to save nations. Their wisdom and favor will allow people to see the love of God through an obedient servant. Even at the end of a kingdom, God will have a man or women like Daniel (as we see in the book of Daniel) saying the truth in the midst of calamities and falling kingdoms.

Daniel was carried away to exile but used God's gifts of prophecy and dream interpretation to guide a nation. The king saw proof that there was only one true God. However, if you recall, the world became jealous because of his gifting. Daniel's enemies, false prophets and seers, lost their social and financial positions. They devised a plan to get rid of Daniel, by going against his honesty and integrity to serve and worship God.

In Daniel 6, God continues to choose men to be his vessels to bring deliverance, financial blessing and peace to the earth. Daniel 1:17, *"As for these four young men, God gave them knowledge and skill in all literature and wisdom; and Daniel had understanding in all visions and dreams."*

When people start recognizing their position rather than their circumstance, God will use their talent. Start volunteering and miracles will start happening, and perhaps you will be one to save an ungodly nation like Daniel or Joseph. Gen 41:40. *"And Pharaoh said to Joseph, "See, I have set you over all the land of Egypt."*

We need more Josephs!

8

GIVING WITH VOLUNTEERS

Each ministry has its own vision, a call to do a Godly action. A business plan that originates in heaven may often look flawed or even impossible to the average businessperson; but the plan by God allows hope to arise and people to see the possibilities of what can supernaturally take place.

God's leaders hear the heart of God, and by faith their actions unlock hearts to give and in so doing 'break the back' of the world market economic forces.

"Without faith it is impossible to please God." Heb 11:6
"Faith without works is dead" James 2:20

Without works you just have dead religion or a social gathering. The faith-walk breaks every world market principle and mind set. Each time through a Godly calling, the principle of GIVING works and we see financial breakthrough. Buildings are constructed, businesses established, organizations thrive, and efforts come to fruition. God's projects are always funded; however, if His people stop following by faith, things start unraveling.

"For God so loved the world he gave his only begotten Son" John 3:16

God established the Lion's Market with man and then with an exclamation point provided the greatest gift: "Jesus". Sometimes Christians think that their giving is a final action, but it is just the start of a blessing. God promised Israel the land, an inheritance and possessions, but it required time and actions for them to receive the finished work.

FIRST THE WORD, THEN THE WORK

The faith walk is a series of volunteer actions (by faith) that accept the gift of opportunities each day. A good example is when you say God gives a child? Hmm, did you have a miraculous conception, or did God allow the natural act of conception to take place? For the gift to take place our actions are required, even after his decrees. Work does not stop after He speaks, it starts!

The Gift of God is eternal life. When did He give the gift? The answer is when He declared the gift, but to enter into it we must die daily (which is completely the opposite of how the world thinks). To fulfill the work of God, it is required that you first believe and then take action. It requires action after a birth to raise a child. So, you see the gift is just the **starting point** for our faith to manifest and deliver God's plans.

"For now, we see through a glass, darkly; but then face to face: now I know in part; but then shall I know even as also I am known." 1 Corinthians 13:12

The Holy Spirit inspires the Apostle Paul to say that we only know in part, but the Lion's Economy brings the unveiling of the GIVING principle in the Saints Movement and it will continue to develop along with the VOLUNTEERING principle. One revelation builds on the other not negating any of the other principles of faith, patience, love and good works. God's principles are ETERNAL.

RESOURCES

How does God supply or resource His works in the Lion's Market? Through a giving people who joyfully volunteer to do His work. A good example is from the Old Testament. Deborah called for volunteers to fight an unwinnable fight against the enemies of Israel. In the book of Judges, we see the people come together and volunteer for the fight.

They had no weapons, they were outnumbered and even the General had to be persuaded to fight. However, the people obeyed God's plan to deliver Israel. And they won! Deborah's song of victory in Judges chapter 5, Verses 8 and 9 says, *"When they chose new gods, war came to the city gates, and not a shield or spear was seen among forty thousand in Israel. My heart is with Israel's princes, with the willing volunteers among the people."*

The Lord's victory because of Deborah's obedience and the people's willingness to volunteer in the face of terrible odds brought forty years of peace to the nation of Israel.

Praise the LORD! God's plans will take place through gifts, giving and volunteers. When Saints obey and follow the word of the Lord then a great desire to volunteer will fall on their hearts. As communities are changed through volunteerism and giving, there will be a renewed fear of the Lord that will take place in the land.

In Chronicles 2:17, Jehoshaphat became king of Judah and God gave him the kingdom through his action to obey God and do His will. In these passages, the leader obeys God and uses volunteers to possess the land and it brings a fear upon his enemies. Hear what God is saying, hear His timing for you. Have faith, trust and be obedient to His word!

"Believe the Lord and you will be established and believe the prophet and you shall prosper." 2 Chronicles 20:20

9

THE ETERNAL ECONOMY

We are an eternal people who will one day will reign as kings and priests

"And have made us kings and priests to our God; And we shall reign on the earth." Revelation 5:10 (NKJV)

Many Christians have no idea that we are destined to be rulers on the earth after the return of Christ.

In Revelations chapter 21 the Apostle John sees a new Heaven and Earth and the new city of Jerusalem descending out of Heaven. Then in verses 21-27, *"The main street of the City was pure gold, translucent as glass. But there was no sign of a Temple, for the Lord God—the Sovereign-Strong—and the Lamb are the Temple."* (The City doesn't need the sun or moon for light. God's Glory is its light, the Lamb its lamp!) **"The nations** will walk in its light and earth's kings will bring in their splendor. Its gates will never be shut by day, and there won't be any night. They'll bring the glory and honor of the nations into the City. Nothing dirty or defiled will get into the City, and no one who defiles or deceives will either. Only those whose names are written in the Lamb's Book of Life will get in."

There will be NATIONS populating the new earth. Did you know that? There will be people and they will have kings and governments and those who have been, and are, followers of Christ will be His rulers and leaders and priests. Think about it! God's plan has always been for this earth to be inhabited and His plan has not changed.

FEEDING THE FOUR THOUSAND

The Gospel of Mark chapter 8 verses 1-9

"During those days another large crowd gathered. Since they had nothing to eat, Jesus called his disciples to him and said, "I have compassion for these people; they have already been with me three days and have nothing to eat. If I send them home hungry, they will collapse on the way, because some of them have come a long distance." His disciples answered, "But where in this remote place can anyone get enough bread to feed them?" "How many loaves do you have?" Jesus asked, "Seven," they replied. He told the crowd to sit down on the ground. When he had taken the seven loaves and given thanks, he broke them and gave them to his disciples to distribute to the people, and they did so. They had a few small fish as well; he gave thanks for them also and told the disciples to distribute them. The people ate and were satisfied. Afterward the disciples picked up seven basketfuls of broken pieces that were left over. About four thousand were present. After he had sent them away."

BEWARE OF THE LEAVEN

In Matthew's account of the same story we see the contrast between earthly and heavenly understanding. Verses 14-21: *"Now the disciples had forgotten to take bread, and they did not have more than one loaf with them in the boat. Then He charged them, saying, "Take heed, beware of the leaven of the Pharisees and the leaven of Herod." And they reasoned among themselves, saying, "It is because we have no bread." But Jesus, being aware of it, said to them, "Why do you reason because you have no bread? Do you not yet perceive nor understand? Is your heart still hardened? Having eyes, do you not see? And having ears, do you not hear? And do you not remember? When I broke the five loaves for the five thousand, how many baskets full of fragments Did you take up?" They said to Him, "Twelve".*

"Also, when I broke the seven for the four thousand, how many large baskets full of fragments did you take up?" And they said, "seven." So, He said to them, "How is it you do not understand?"

The Lord Jesus must have been at least a little frustrated with the disciples. He was trying to get them to see such an important truth. The Pharisees and Herod basically controlled the national economy. They were operating completely 'in the flesh' with no concern for others and especially eternity. They ruled for only themselves and typify the leaders of the present World Market and throughout history.

I'm sensing the Lord calling for the Church to pick up the mantle of GIVING; not hoarding for self-interest and self-preservation. And our giving should start with our LOVE.
"So, he answered and said, "You shall love the LORD your God with all your heart, with all your soul, with all your strength, and with all your mind,' and 'your neighbor as yourself." Luke 10:27

FALSE GIVERS

Sadly, there will be those who will be false believers who will try to be a part of the Lion's Market. We see this plainly in the sad account of Ananias and his wife Sapphira.

"But a certain man named Ananias, with Sapphira his wife, sold a possession. And he kept back part of the proceeds, his wife also being aware of it, and brought a certain part and laid it at the apostles' feet (implying that it was the entire amount from the sale). But Peter said, "Ananias, why has Satan filled your heart to lie to the Holy Spirit and keep back part of the price of the land for yourself? While it remained, was it not your own? And

after it was sold, was it not in your own control? Why have you conceived this thing in your heart? You have not lied to men but to God." Acts 5: 1

We must take care to do our giving in purity and with right motives and spirit. We should all be giving freely with happy and glad hearts our money, talent and time.

ECONOMICS

Economics is the social science that studies the production, distribution, and consumption of goods and services. The term economics comes from the Ancient Greek οἰκονομία (oikonomia, "management of a household, administration") from οἶκος (oikos, "house") + νόμος (nomos, "custom" or "law"), hence "rules of the house(hold)".

Lionel Robbins (London School of Economics) wrote, "the science which studies human behavior as a relationship between ends and scarce means which have alternative uses." Scarcity means that available resources are insufficient to satisfy all wants and needs.

Absent scarcity and alternative uses of available resources, there is no economic problem. The subject thus defined involves the study of choices by individuals who may represent a population whose position of authority/power/influence gives them the means to affect an economy.

The keys for analysis here are human behavior economics and household management when you study economics. So, a Lion's Market or World Market is defined by individual choices. For each personal choice we make, God holds us responsible and for them we will be judged.

The Church can dictate final outcomes if we choose. We can reward those who are benefiting the community and we can encourage those who are not to change their business practices. Many say we cannot impact the economy, but we do every day. We must as Christians obey Godly economic principles and not negate our priestly role.

SCARCITY

We now know that the economic problem is a scarcity of resources and their distribution to the population. We as Christians must take up and apply God's principles to this paradigm, the principle of giving as a market force to change the world. What are the needs and wants of society? What should be produced and distributed? Are the goods insufficient to satisfy all needs? So, looking at the Lion's Market economic model, we can help solve the economic problem of "Scarcity."

Capitalism, Socialism and Communism are terms used to identify how a system controls the manufacture of products (supply) and its methods to control demand. The Lion's Market economic model is laid out plainly in the Scriptures:

"The earth is the Lord's and the fullness therein." PS 24:1
"I will supply all your needs according to my riches in glory" Philippians 4:19

"'The silver is mine and the gold is mine,' declares the Lord Almighty." Haggai 2:8

God declares and reminds us that there is another economic system, an everlasting one. God himself is the source of supply. Through Him and His people all lack could be diminished. Divine distribution of resources, services or goods is through God's people.

GIVING

So, the Lion's Market has a central controlling factor and it is a Market Principle called GIVING.

The Bible says, *"Give, and it will be given to you: good measure, pressed down, shaken together, and running over will be put into your bosom. For with the same measure that you use, it will be measured back to you."* Luke 6:38

Supply and Demand is the major factor in any Economic Theory or paradigm of discussion. I use the word paradigm because when you study economics, experts expand and define what is Supply (Production, Goods, Services, Resources) while Demand (Consumption) is the Need or Want of (Production, Goods, Services, Resources). However, the bottom line when looking at individuals is the question "How much is enough?"

To one person a 10,000 sq. ft. home with eight bedrooms is barely sufficient for shelter, while to another a 1,300 sq. ft., three-bedroom home is a palace. Understanding that there are differing and very subjective scales of need (home, food and shelter) is very important.

Just because someone has more, or less, than their neighbor does not define how Godly, blessed, holy or righteous a person or family is or isn't. It can in instances reveal a work-ethic, character or faith-walk but it is subject to the individual view of what is enough for shelter, food, security and clothing.

TWO ILLUSTRATIONS

A factory was built in a South American country. Local people were trained and hired for the new jobs and the community was blessed with more employment opportunities.

The new factory was producing low-cost products and using low-cost labor which would allow the factory to be profitable. The workers received their first pay check after two weeks on the job, and the following Monday none of them returned to work. Why? The workers were paid enough that it was enough for a whole year, so why go to work?

Their needs were met! Their view of abundant life was not defined by the same wants as others and they did not consider any future needs. Their time, wealth, and security were met and that was sufficient for them.

The second story is about the collectibles fad for Beanie Babies stuffed toys et al. A production and consumption of a product for what? People paid and even today pay high prices for these 'toys', go figure?! You can't eat it, wear it, take shelter in it, it can't protect you, and it will not last very long without proper care.

A product is created and marketed and for some reason a compulsive need spreads through a population driving up demand and prices for a product with no real purpose.

Each story is a picture of ways the dysfunctional World Market works based on individual needs and wants. We must always remember that so long as we are 'in this world' those operating by its (the World's) economic rules will never understand the Eternal Economy.

10

DEMAND

When you meet someone do you ever find yourself wondering what they WANT? Some see the word 'demand' in today's usage as haughty or sacrilegious but by true definition, it is **'an insistence or request made, as if by right'.**

The word 'demand' used as a noun puts TRUTH at the forefront of our actions. It requires us to take a militaristic and unapologetic stand for truth. Truth is eternal and deals not only with today's issues but also looks to the future providing vision so that Godly reform will happen. Holy Spirit motivated and directed Demands reveal our desires, appetites and wants which are Lion's Market economic generators that line up with the Truth.

"..and Godly fear is the beginning of wisdom." John 17:17

"The fear of the Lord is the beginning of knowledge: but fools despise wisdom and instruction." Proverbs 1:7

"The fear of the Lord is the beginning of wisdom: and the knowledge of the holy is understanding." Proverbs 9:10

DEMAND CREATES MOMENTUM

Demand also creates a foundation for future actions, "a series of demands". It creates a momentum for far-reaching reforms that can subdue the world's kingdoms. We are able to insist (demand) by right through the revealed Logos and Rhema Word (Truth) of God.

Look at the synonyms of demand: request, call, command, order, dictate, ultimatum, stipulation. These are key words that are used by radical reformists and activists today. God spoke the world into existent with a 'demand', "Let there be.." The call of God puts a demand on the truth that is living within us to stand, occupy and fight for the project that GOD HAS CALLED US TO in this life.

Men and women today can have a call/demand to establish a church, half-way house, orphanage, feeding center, school, drug rehab or other ministry of hope with a right to reform their community. Men and women are called to be teachers, lawyers, scientists, etc. When we line up with God's will, our wishes, desires, and wants to become His expression to the world. We become the 'hands and voice of God' with our activities and actions.

THE ECONOMICS

The desires or wants of purchasers, consumers, clients, employers, etc., for a commodity, service, or other item provides strong impetus in both the World and the Lion's Markets. The Lion's Market exchange tender is Faith, and if not present will create a 'slump' in the Market. Little faith produces fewer 'products' and results in little market movement. When there was little faith or a lack of faith only a few miracles and works were done in Jesus' time.
The source of faith is God and He says, "I will supply all your needs according to My riches in glory". There is no need for exchange rates, it is equal in all 'provinces' because there is one Kingdom. The scripture also reads, "without faith it is impossible to please God". **Faith initiates the Law of Supply and Demand in the Lion's Market.** He uses men and women as His supply lines to provided 'products' for His people. Lion's Market Products are the results of our faith-actions.

Much of the world measures someone's wealth only by their possessions. It is sad that many 'worldly' Christians do this also. Our true 'Value' is what <u>remains at death,</u> so decay and corruption cannot destroy it. As Christians, we should only measure worth by the value of Godly works that remain, that testify to our faith. **God says faith without works is dead.** No Products = No Faith.

The value of a faith product is measured by love. The Bible teaches "faith, hope, and love will remain" along with the Word. You cannot show your faith acts without "these signs that shall follow them that believe".

THE MATH

If you show me your works, I will show you my faith. When I see your works, I can measure your faith. If you are a 'salesman' of Faith, then you are using the currency to unveil different products of faith. A minister of faith that demonstrates the 'products' of faith can be judged by love.

*"And though I have the gift of prophecy, and understand all mysteries and all knowledge, and though I have **all faith** so that I could remove mountains, but have not love, I am nothing. (like Balam). And though I bestow all my goods to feed the poor, and though I give my body to be burned, but have not love, it **profits me nothing.** "*1 Corinthians 13:2-3

Your life ministry could result in nothing! You may have faith but without using it IN LOVE you could gain the whole world and still lose your soul. Some ministers today are using the principle of faith, but they have forgotten their first love.

So, the Lion's Market 'Law of Supply and Demand' works differently than the World's Market. **The Faith to believe His Word and act in LOVE is the key the Lion's Market and eternal success.** "*Faith comes by hearing, and hearing by the Word of God.*" Romans 10:8

"*... through faith in His name, has made this man strong, whom you see and know. Yes, the faith which comes through Him has given him this perfect soundness in the presence of you all.* " Acts 3:16

ONLY FAITH (with LOVE) FULFILLS DEMAND

Only Faith and the works that are initiated and executed by it result in 'products' of eternal value. Faith comes by hearing the WORD of God, either or both the Rhema or Logos Word of God. Faith can be seen, measured and proportioned.

__Through Christians' Faithfulness in operating in faith with love, blessings from God will flow into and through their lives and into those in their community. How much faith we choose to exercise in our lives can have a tremendous effect today and in eternity.__

11
THE TREASURY

BUILDING SUPPLY LINES

In the Lion's Market, the consumption of goods and services take place as God's works manifest through believers obediently walking in faith in every area of their lives. The Treasury in God's economy is God's people.

"The earth is the Lord's and the fullness therein." Psalms 24:1

When God wants an assignment or a task to be accomplished we will say that He supplies the need. That sounds well and good but how does He do it? Wire transfer from heaven? Treasure chest appearing on our front porch? In reality, we understand that He speaks to the hearts of His people, His 'Treasury' to fund His projects.

The Christians in today's world possess/control more wealth than all the world markets combined. Trillions of dollars are at the fingertips of God through His people. He builds the supply lines and coordinates resources for distribution.

NEW TESTAMENT FINANCIAL SUPPORT

In the following scriptures, we see how God used people to finance the work of the ministry. Some believe that this only applies to work in the church or directly related to the church ie. ministers, missionaries, preachers etc. but we see how the Lord blesses faithful people with abundance and prosperity SO THAT they can fund heaven's works here on the earth.

"*After this, Jesus traveled from one city and village to another. He spread the Good News about God's kingdom. The twelve apostles were with him. Also, some women were with him. They had been cured from evil spirits and various illnesses. These women were Mary, also called Magdalene, from whom seven demons had gone out;* **Joanna, whose husband Chusa was Herod's administrator; Susanna; and many other women. They provided financial support for Jesus and his disciples.**" Luke 8:1-3

"*Moreover, as you Philippians know, in the early days of your acquaintance with the gospel, when I set out from Macedonia, not one church shared with me in the matter of giving and receiving, except you only; for even when I was in Thessalonica,* **you sent me aid more than once when I was in need**. *Not that I desire your gifts; what I desire is that more be credited to your account. I have received full payment and have more than enough. I am amply supplied, now that I have received from Epaphroditus the gifts you sent. They are a fragrant offering, an acceptable sacrifice, pleasing to God. And my God will meet all your needs according to the riches of his glory in Christ Jesus. To our God and Father be glory for ever and ever. Amen.*" Philippians 4:15-20

God's work will take place as he taps into the hearts of His people. If funds appear to dry up he will unlock the storehouses of the earth (His people) to fund His projects. The production of wealth will continue to take place as God moves on His people to have insight, wisdom, and innovation in business. God in this last reformation will continue to raise up his sheep to feed the world.

COVENANT HOUSE, THE BEGINNING

Sometimes we forget that our actions following the revealing of God's destiny and call on our life can be critically important. A group home that some refer to as a halfway house is a great example of following God's call on your life. Wilbur and Mary Linda Butts received a call to start such a home. This occurred after Wilbur in his mid-forty's finally got saved. Mary Linda had prayed for years but Wilbur was in rebellion but finally God said to him 'now or never' in one last call in church. Wilbur confessed that God gave him this last choice.

Just knowing about God is not sufficient, you must accept his call and finally Wilbur said yes. Not too long after that God spoke to the couple about devoting their lives to developing a halfway house for men and women who needed help for a second chance in life. After much praying the couple started looking for a home and someone mentioned an old hotel built in 1935 by a paper company.

The place looked not only dilapidated but like you should just bulldoze it. Most of its windows were missing glass, the roof leaked like a sieve and the flooring was rotted. Where most people saw no potential Wilbur and Mary Linda saw a future home for twenty residents. As Wilbur met with the owner they agreed on a price that God had given to Wilbur as the purchase price of over ninety thousand dollars and he wanted a down payment. Wilbur said they had no dollars, but he agreed to write a check for $2,500. The owner agreed that would be sufficient to hold the property until finances were achieved.

The problem was they had no dollars for the down payment or the mortgage. They had the vision but where will the money come from? First God moved that day to cover the check through a meeting in town after someone heard about the vision for the home. Second, as a couple Wilbur and Mary Linda agreed to sell their home and invest everything into God's plan.

What seemed as an impossible job (fixing up the broken-down property) became do-able as men showed up at the home and a contractor said' 'we can conquer this task'. They had a steel building donated to them they just had to tear it down, and that became the homes new roof. Another person donated an old skating rink which they used for a 'new' tongue and grooved floor.

As time went on donations came through that allowed the restoration to continue. What seemed impossible became possible because twenty-five men volunteering their time revealed that paint, wood work and great talent can solve what money can't buy. Work step by step, use what God gives you and He will make a way.

As buildings were given to them and the talents of many men, most of whom would be considered 'castaways' used their abilities and what seemed impossible became possible! Carpenter skills, tile skills, cabinet making skills, and HVAC skills were all a part of the new residents sent or who found their way to that home.

This home today is clear example of a call on a person life and how willing hearts to volunteer can change the lives of people, families and whole communities. A home that anyone else would have demolished became a jewel in the woods. People giving, and volunteering is the key to the Covenant House today.

Lion's Market principles is how it was created and exists and has a future. Have faith and step out with the vision God has given you!

12

THE SEVEN MOUNTAINS

RIGHTEOUS CREATIVE INNOVATIVE

The Seven Mountain Principles, as popularized by Lance Walnau, is a great revelation for today's believers. We see God developing leaders and 'influencers' across the spheres of business, family, education, religion, finance, entertainment, and media. These seven mountains are subsets of the Lion's Market that can affect supply and demand.

Each of the seven mountains transition to an everlasting market that does not implode every 50 years like the World Market.
Each works on the principle of GIVING and truth. How can you over-accumulate when you find joy in giving? Holy Spirit led leaders have the means to bring tremendous influence within their sphere based on their assignment from God which is the application of a market-based system that is honest, truthful, and giving.

This is very different if not actually the opposite of the business and even church structure that we see today (sad!). The seven mountain principles require a unified kingdom force employed by leaders that eliminates and enforces; no bribery, no corruption, no immorality, and no bloodshed among government, business and clergy. The Godly kingdom leaders will use this wisdom to fight poverty and lack that are rampant in what we know as the secular systems (world market).

INTEGRITY = PROPSPERITY

The world population would be blessed in every culture and country if dishonesty, immorality, and corruption were stopped. The secular world cannot manage this themselves because of its foundation of self-interest.

Today's lukewarm seeker-sensitive 'churches' cannot manage to bring righteous transformation because they don't represent Christ and His true Church. Self-interest is also their goal; however, God is rising up leaders that will be faithful like Daniel. True godly leaders who will be like John the Baptist, and Moses. They will not waiver in the correct way to judge and will hear God on how to prevent economic disasters.

True, Spirit-led Church leaders will not lie, cheat and solely focus on their own social agendas. Today many church leaders will say that they teach truth and honesty, but then tell their parishioners that everyone else lies and that honesty is subjective. Many also preach and teach that EVERYONE is going to heaven because the Bible says that we aren't supposed to judge. That is heresy.

THE CHURCH FIRST

The Bible says that Judgment must take place FIRST in the house of God (1Pet 4:17). The church of this world has lost its 'saltiness' and can no longer preserve. The true Church made up of many members is different because they are traveling in the of WAY of Holiness. The Path to Life is narrow and requires true and honest living that is pleasing to God, not man.

Jesus is the Ruler and God is the Judge and He requires His people and especially those in leadership to have an upright heart. When you work as a Christian in a secular job everyone should be able to point to you as a person having an honest and righteous lifestyle. If you are trying to measure by your own guidelines you will come up lacking. We only have one standard, and that is a person, Jesus Christ!

Godly leaders will use the Bible and prayer as their guide. This will bring prosperity and peace when applied systemically throughout all their policies and actions. Truthfulness is the goal to be achieved with great endurance and perseverance. Is it always popular? No, but the ability to achieve the highest goal is always best to bring correction to a life that is out of alignment.

Truthfulness is not double-mindedness as it reads in James 1:8 *"A double-minded man is unstable in ALL of their ways"*. The world stumbles like a drunken man in need of finding the true path. God says there is only one way, Christ Jesus and only He can provide guidance for a world system that has long lost a true moral compass.

> ***No matter what Mountain you are called to, you are called to influence those around you and to be an example of Christ's life.***

13

GIVE ME MY MOUNTAIN

Let's Look at an example where God used the old adage 'When life gives you lemons make lemonade'. Abraham and Lot had a dispute over resources, but God had a plan.
"So Abram said to Lot, "Please let there be no strife between you and me, and between my herdsmen and your herdsmen; for we are brethren. Is not the whole land before you? Please separate from me. If you take the left, then I will go to the right; or, if you go to the right, then I will go to the left." Genesis 13:8

Abraham's blessing was assigned by God. Abraham wanted peace and said to Lot '(you) choose that we may have peace'. Resources were scarce, but Abraham knew God would provide. As the account unfolds we see that Lot choose to move to where he thought it was the best in man's eyes. The land of Jordan, where water and grasses were plentiful and the best place for sheep and goats to be raised.

So, Abraham dwelt in Canaan, but in reality, he stayed in the land that God had called him to. This is an example because it brings out two kinds of results. The peace and the blessing of God are irrevocable when you go where God calls you. God will bless you in the place he assigns you, even though resources might seem inadequate at times.

APPEARANCES CAN DECIEVE

Lot did not follow God's commandments, but Abraham followed the call of God in his life. He was blessed because he followed God. Even though the territory was more rugged it did not matter because he was righteous in his steps. Lot chose what the world would judge because of perceived benefit. Lot is an example of the world system and what will happen to man when righteousness and morals do not prevail in the land.

"He has given food and provision to those who reverently and worshipfully fear Him; He will remember His covenant forever and imprint it [on His mind]. He has declared and shown to His people the power of His works in giving them the heritage of the nations [of Canaan]. The works of His hands are [absolute] truth and justice [faithful and right]; and all His decrees and precepts are sure (fixed, established, and trustworthy)." Psalm 111:5-7 (Amplified Bible)

"And not being weak in faith, he did not consider his own body, already dead (since he was about a hundred years old), and the deadness of Sarah's womb. He did not waver at the promise of God through unbelief, but was strengthened in faith, giving glory to God, 21 and being fully convinced that what He had promised He was also able to perform." Romans 4:19-21 (NKJV)

WHAT IS YOUR MOUNTAIN?

Mine was healthcare in a small rural county that was broken. As a born-again Christian, I had an assignment of God to a position (possession). In 1998 I had positioned myself in the Healthcare Marketplace to be qualified as a County Health Officer over a small rural county. At that time not too, many Health Officers were administrators but doctors. The State Department of Health was changing, and new positions could be filled by MPH qualified candidates.

Having previously worked under seven doctors and recognizing a good challenge, I applied for the job with thoughtful prayer. The community and many friends came to my aide to put a good word in for my cause to the State DOH and Governor's office.

However, the doctor over me stopped in one day and said she was not going to recommend me and if any other letters of recommendation came in she was going to fire me. At this moment I asked God what do you and want me to do what do you want me to say? Out of my mouth came the following statement; "I have worked for seven Directors and they all have stood in front of my desk as they were leaving and informed me of the great job I had done for them and I said the eighth one if it happens will feel no different, however you missed the best chance to have the best Administrator this County will ever have".

Well, I went home that day and said to my wife that if the Lord wants me to have the job he would have to give it to me because she was not going to recommend me for it. So, in eight weeks after being appointed acting Administrator, the same supervising doctor came back and said, "I am going to recommend you for the job."

POSSESSING YOUR MOUNTAIN

That was over thirteen years ago. and God has allowed favor to grow in people's hearts so that when God gave me a project it became successful with His guidance. Bottom line: I could not have accomplished all that has occurred unless partnership and people recognized the need and the unselfish desire to do what was right.

That little Health Department has developed over the years from a department that did minimal public health programs to a vital health infrastructure for the community. We went from just having immunizations, birth control facilities and community disease surveillance to now having two full-time MD's, 4 Nurse Practitioners, 2 Dentists and a LCSW (Licensed Clinical Social Worker). Praise God!

This established 2 full-time medical centers with General Dentistry for the community. Along with all of this came Mental Health and a countywide School Health program. We became the 1st Health Department that integrated a community Health Center in Public Health in Florida. We went from 12 employees to 80 employees and are now one of the largest employers in the County.

God revealed how people with little or no means to pay could get access to quality healthcare. God provided people to help write grants with me and we now have the only real-time digital x-ray in the surrounding counties. We went from a $750,000 budget to a $4M budget!

God created an economic generator that provided discounts for patients based on their income. Real-time 21st Century medicine was reaching all residents regardless of their ability to pay. What most people deemed as impossible God gave me a vision for the possibility. Giving, expecting nothing in return other than doing what was right was the true test.

There are so many things I could share about, like how God provided a top-notch women's center and grants but that would take many more paragraphs. I think you can see that God provided favor but I had to work with righteousness. He was my CEO and projects were subject to honesty, fairness and truth. This resulted in blessing a whole community rather than just enriching a few at the top.

When God shows you the 'Mountain' that you are to possess, no matter how impossible it may seem, HAVE FAITH! Like Abraham, even when everyone else chooses what seems right in the eyes of the world you stay the course that the Holy Spirit has shown you and the Lord will provide His Favor, Resources and the People you need to take that MOUNTAIN for the Glory of God!

14

STEWARDSHIP

How does 'Stewardship' take place in the Lion's Market?

This is a question that can be best answered when you look at how the term was used in the Bible. In passages throughout the Gospels we see mention of stewards as managers of property and taking care of another person's financial affairs, business or household. They have no ownership but are entrusted to rightly manage the affairs of the owner.

So, an interchangeable word for 'steward' in today's understanding is 'manager'. It is a term that could be used in the marketplace for supervisor, administrator, executive or director. However, as in the Gospels, we see the danger and resulting negative impact of complacency in a manager or steward.
Managers who are selfish, lazy, criminal or just incompetent waste resources and can bankrupt a business.

We see horrible examples of bad management in today's stock and hedge funds. Bernie Madoff is infamous for his fleecing of investors close to 65 BILLION dollars. The executives of Enron lost their investors 60 Billion dollars with total disregard for the individual investors they are supposed to work for.

In our government we see purchases of $150 hammers and no- bid contracts going to friends or relatives again with NO REGARD for the taxpayers. In the mortgage backed securities debacle we saw how private business that works only for self-interest lost more dollars and crippled the world economy more than any other incident in recent history.

Integrity, honesty, trustworthiness, generosity and selflessness are all hallmarks of a Steward in the Lion's Market.

So, what is our steward or management role in the Lion's Market? According to Gospels in the parable of the Talents we see the owner (God) expects a return and a profit. We must accept as Christians that God the Father is the true owner of ALL our possessions.

We are stewards or managers and have been entrusted by Him and will be held accountable. We will be held responsible for its use and the distribution of resources. Financial and resource management is not an option, it is a requirement. The Father does expect a return and when the great white throne judgment occurs, and God will be looking at what we did with all that he gave us charge of, be it small or large.

You may be thinking God will let me slide on into heaven without asking and demanding accountability, but this would be opposite of the parable of the talents, we may think we own our business, home, money, but as Christians 100% of our assets are His.
Tithes (10%) should be given for the work of the church but the other 90% is also subject to use by the Holy Spirit.

THE TITHE PRINCIPAL

The Tithe principle was laid down before the Mosaic Law and was acknowledge when Paul explained that Abraham gave tithes to a priest Melchizedek before the Law.

"And Melchizedek king of Shalem brought out bread and wine; now he was a priest of God Most High. And he blessed him and said, "Blessed be Abram of God Most High, possessor of heaven and earth; and blessed be God Most High, who has delivered your enemies into your hand." And he gave him a tenth of all." Hebrews 7: 1,2 referencing Genesis 14:18-20

Melchizedek is translated as King of Righteousness Lord has sworn and will not change His mind, *"Thou art a priest forever according to the order of Melchizedek."* Psalm 110:4

So, we see that funding of the ministry is one from the heart of giving not by ordinance but of grace. Abraham was an example of a priesthood of the promise and tithe was from the heart not law. In the book of Malachi, we see that we rob God through withholding tithes and offerings but in the New Covenant we see Jesus praising a widow who gave a mite, everything she had in contrast to the wealthy making a big deal out of their offerings.

God loves a cheerful giver. The widow was not rebuked for giving such a small amount which in fact was all that she had but was praised for what she gave to God. It was never discussed how the temple was using her money nor was it discussed that she should stop giving to a corrupt synagogue. God expects us to use His guidance to plant us in a covenant church of ministry. Then we need to give our support and I believe it is at least 10%. We are held accountable to give but the biggest responsibility lays on the leadership. The ministry is funded by tithes and it is a no-brainier on what to do with our first 10% of income.

What is surprising after being involved in churches for over 35 years is that only about 20% of members in a congregation actually pay tithes. How about the 90% leftover since God provides excellent examples on why to tithe. As God got my attention and said the 10% will be for the priesthood but the 90% I will be responsible and accountable for.

On this thought I feel like we need to fear and tremble and be wise with God's resources. As Steward and manager of these funds and resources God will expect a return! Remember the parable of the vineyard where the master of the house sent his son for his share. In the Great White Throne Judgment God will expect His return. So as resource managers we must be wise with God's resources.

TIME AND MONEY

Two of our most important God-given resources are time and money. In reality, money and time are directly related. Salaries and money represent a prorated portion of our time. Personal time represents great value for the many different skill talents in the body of Christ. When a work is to be established then God pulls from his people money, tangible resources and work skills. This volunteer spirit manifests as a Godly desire to give of our resources and make the work of God come to pass.

The Holy Spirit takes our stewardship with money, resources and labor to fulfill his outreach to world. Most projects led by the Holy Spirit will be completed at 75% of the cost in real-world dollars and at the end in most cases have no debt. I'm not saying debt-free since I find God providing new visions to expand his Church and that can require ongoing financing. The resource manager is really God who uses the Holy Spirit to move on his people to provide.

A TRUE STORY

A good example of a stewardship project is how God can orchestrate a project without all parties knowing the cost. I participated in a group home expansion project in moving a house built in 1870's. The home was being used as a bank, but the bank wanted the structure moved and replaced with a new branch.

The Covenant House leaders, Wilbur and Mary Linda Butts wanted to bid and purchase the home by moving the structure to their property thus expanding their housing for residents. The banks intent was to receive bids for the home and it be moved.

The home leaders, Wilbur Butts and Walter Fields were going to bid but a stop-order arose when God instructed Wilbur that he could not. Even though the Covenant House had a need and had performed smaller projects similar they could not bid. They were planning to purchase the house and hire a house moving company. The bank knew of the Covenant House interest and was delighted that such a fine structure would go to a worthy cause if they were chosen as the lowest bidder. However, on the day of bidding, the bank noticed there was no bid from them.

When Wilbur was called he had to tell them that God had instructed them not bid on the project. The bank continued and awarded the bid to highest bidder. There were several bidders at the opening however in couple of weeks all backed out. The bank then found out it was going to cost them $14,000 to demolishing the structure and clean up the property.

During this time period Wilbur and Walt heard the news and God instructed them to talk to bank. Wilbur called the bank and asked if they moved the home would the bank give them $14,000. The bank came back and said to Wilbur we will give you the monies to demolish the home if you do it in 30 days.

This was a enormous structure which was a three story wood type home and 10,000 sq ft. Wilbur and Mary Linda with Walt had an assignment from God. The bank was now going pay them rather than them paying for the move. Then God gave favor in the community who heard of the project and many of the local church denominations and other Christians started helping. A Mennonite brother loaned a lowboy and truck. Another individual supplied a small Crane and the local hardware store provided credit.

The Covenant House was housing 25 residents and all of them went to work. Like a jigsaw puzzle it was dismantled and marked as the home was taken apart from the roof down. All items were saved even the landscaping. All bricks and lumber were saved so the building could be completely rebuilt. In other words, in 28 days the structure was removed, the landscaped removed and the lot leveled by a loaned bulldozer and truck.

What would have cost over $400,000 cost only thousands! God moved on His people to supply what was needed. This is the Lion's Market example at work.

Presently the house is erected and houses residents. God made space available to help the unwanted who got an opportunity to know Him. What was impossible in the world market was possible through giving and volunteers in the Lion's Market!

Praise God!

15

WANTS

'Wants' are based on the desire to have but that has no bearing as to whether they will be beneficial. Look at all the stuff in your garage. At one time you wanted it all but now it is just sitting there gathering dust.

One of the assumptions made in economics and the methods which attempt to solve the economic problem is that humans are generally greedy. Thus, the market takes advantage of these appetites and produces as much as possible to satisfy them.

Things such as food and clothing can be classified as either wants or needs, depending on what type of goods they are and how often they are consumed/used. God has said He would 'supply all our needs according to His riches in glory' but how about our wants?

MOSES LAID IT OUT

In Deuteronomy chapter 28 we see that God has a plan and desire to bless His children and supply our wants. Assuming the same principles apply today for the Church as it did for the children of Israel we can be blessed, pressed down, shaken together and running over.

Also, in Deuteronomy chapter 28 we see blessing declared by God for food, shelter, family and for the protection against enemies. All their needs and many common wants filled. God's basic principle to avoid lack is found in verse 1 "hearken diligently to His voice and obey His commandments."

Today, many don't read God's word and they either don't know that they can hear His voice, or they don't want to. Thus, the blessing in verse 1 is given up and the judgments revealed further on in the chapter occur.

Because thou servedst not the LORD thy God with joyfulness, and with gladness of heart, for the abundance of all things; Therefore shalt thou serve thine enemies which the LORD shall send against thee, in hunger, and in thirst, and in nakedness, and in want of all things: and he shall put a yoke of iron upon thy neck, until he have destroyed thee." Deuteronomy 28:47

So, the world market economic problem fundamentally revolves around the idea of choice. Due to the limited resources available, businesses must determine what to produce first to satisfy demand. How can the choice be right if we are not obeying Deuteronomy 28:1 by taking heed to God's voice?

Joshua said, "Choose this day whom you are going to serve." If we are serving the God Most High, then we will be making correct choices. And changing the world!

16
PLACE OF THE CHURCH

The church regardless of organizational size has an economic principle that should govern the supply of the ministry. When you look at the Old Testament the priests were supplied by tithes and offerings. This principle remains for today.

When you look at the first church in Acts, the principle applied. The apostles needed to be focused on God's call and work, and in the book of Acts, we see how the first church supplied the apostles and prophets for the work of the ministry.

Though the principle still applies today, we have put the world system into the church. You hear it every day, "we need to run this church like a business." We can run a church as if it is a business but, in that case, we need to run it according to God's principles rather than the false economic model of the worlds. Every church should run 1st on God's assignment, 2nd on faith, 3rd on the principle of giving and 4th volunteerism all of which are the framework of true ministry.

Not only did the early church take care of those in ministry they also looked after the many needs in the body of believers. In the book of Acts, we see that there was a dispute over the care of widows and orphans and in Acts 11 and Corinthians 2:8 they took up the 'grace of giving' for a suffering church that was hurting because of a drought.

A 'TAXING' TIME

Great wealth lies within the church. Trillions of dollars are at God's command. He can roar, and the Lion's Market will go into action. Many needs will be met as God orchestrates funds for his work. However, there is storm cloud arising. It has become clear to me and others that church organizations in America will be attacked within the next 10 years and be required to pay income tax or a special tax on their resources and real property.

You say, 'there is no way that would ever happen, what about the freedom of religion?' There is one fact you may not know. There is more wealth wrapped up churches and not-for-profits than any other businesses in the US. With taxes going up for the middle class, the not-for-profits are the last wealth-frontier which can be taxed to pay for government programs.

It will be said that the churches don't do very much to help their communities considering all of the wealth they possess. Churches will be accused of hoarding. People will say "Why should they be given a tax-exempt status?" Especially with all their abuses of wealth storage.

Sure enough, many not-for-profits are mega businesses with all types of holdings that are not ministry related. With the government continuing to add to its already staggering debt, trillions of dollars will be requested from the organizations. It will start with non-related ministry businesses like housing, malls, restaurants and then progress to all ministry incomes.

Church and non-profit contribution tax deductions will stop or be greatly diminished. This is the very reason we will need dependency and sharing with Godly conviction in supplying goods, housing food and clothing for those in need.

In the new Lion's Market, we will see the basic principles of God's laws being established. You may ask why should they be established? The reason is the past market principles will not apply in today's changing economic system. Presently, the world market cannot project a future growth or direction. Many safe havens for investments will destabilize and some fall. Surety will no longer be available in the stock market.

RETURN TO THE GATE

I believe that in the coming days the legal courts will not be a place of justice for God's people. Basic economic justice will not apply for all and it will be necessary for true economic principles found in the Bible to arise.

In Old Testament times 'court' was held at a city's gate. The elders would gather there, and people could come for wisdom and help with issues and grievances.

True leadership, not that which is corrupted, would provide ways to divide private property and settle disputes. Leadership and true Godly council were the keys in the Old Testament. Is this possible today? I would say the church will return to a system of elders who will help guide the body in the last days. Wise counsel and judgment are no more than arbitration in today's court system.

Godly council could provide for rulings on the proper amounts of interest on debt and other legal matters such as property and monetary compensation concerning property damage. Many teachings in the Old Testament could apply today with Godly leadership. Other occurrences, like personal injury or fines for 'wrongdoing' and compensation in money for various infractions of formalized law. I can see God's people going to a no-usury system and even proclaiming years of Jubilee!

17

YEAR OF JUBILEE

"'Count off seven sabbath years—seven times seven years—so that the seven sabbath years amount to a period of forty-nine years. Then have the trumpet sounded everywhere on the tenth day of the seventh month; on the Day of Atonement sound the trumpet throughout your land. Consecrate the fiftieth year and proclaim liberty throughout the land to all its inhabitants. It shall be a jubilee for you; each of you is to return to your family property and to your own clan. The fiftieth year shall be a jubilee for you; do not sow and do not reap what grows of itself or harvest the untended vines. For it is a jubilee and is to be holy for you; eat only what is taken directly from the fields. In this Year of Jubilee everyone is to return to their own property." Leviticus 25:8-13

Debts were ended, and the liberty of every man was returned. This year of Jubilee is to remind us of the price God paid for us through Jesus who bore the cost of our freedom. What would the world think about a system that regularly brought freedom?
Greed would be controlled, and we would not need the courts, or the money market and God's work would be supported.

We are so materially minded we say this would be impossible. But it worked for hundreds of years and could work even today. I believe we see parts of the system working today within the Jewish society as well as the Amish and Mennonite Societies. No usury and leadership guidance to prevent ownership by the world system.

It is time for the church to function as a beacon of light or to be the salt. I see these societies building houses for each other and controlling their worlds. However, I'm calling on the church to use these Godly principles to impact the world by example and deed.

In our evangelical outreach, new Christians should see that we not only live in the religious mountain but the other six mountains. All parts of the world system such as financial, business, etc. can be solved with Godly leaders and this will allow for peace and safety. The abundance of both material goods and spiritual wealth will be an example to the world. The pressures of the world will be diminished, and lives will have much greater meaning.

The Jubilee statutes tell us to beware of covetousness, 'for a man's life consists not in the abundance of his possessions'. We are to exercise willing dependence on God's providence for our support; to consider ourselves the Lord's tenants or stewards, and to use our possessions accordingly.

SABBATH YEAR

"The Lord said to Moses at Mount Sinai, "Speak to the Israelites and say to them: 'When you enter the land I am going to give you, the land itself must observe a sabbath to the Lord. For six years sow your fields, and for six years prune your vineyards and gather their crops. But in the seventh year, the land is to have a year of sabbath rest, a sabbath to the Lord. Do not sow your fields or prune your vineyards. Do not reap what grows of itself or harvest the grapes of your untended vines. The land is to have a year of rest. Whatever the land yields during the sabbath year will be food for you—for yourself, your male and female servants, and the hired worker and temporary resident who live among you, as well as for your livestock and the wild animals in your land. Whatever the land produces may be eaten." Leviticus 25: 1-7

This Sabbath 'year of rest' typified the spiritual rest which all believers can enter into, through Christ Jesus. Through Him we are eased of the burden of worldly care and labor, both being sanctified and sweetened to us and, we are enabled and encouraged to live by faith.

Jesus declared that He is Lord of the Sabbath. He lives inside of each and every believer and we all should be seeking to allow His perfect peace and rest to be a part of our everyday lives.

18
CONNECTIONS AND RELATIONSHIPS

In the book of Genesis' account of the creation, God declared seven times 'it is good'. In chapter three He states that *"It is not good for man to dwell alone."* This shows that God knew the importance of relationships, with our wife and others. This is the struggle of mankind, to want independence while in fact, God created us to be dependent.

Some avoid at all cost to seek dependence, but we find the best results in partnering with others. In the ancient account of the Tower of Babel God saw that with a common language and like- mindedness man could do whatever they set their minds to.

"Then they said, "Come, let us build ourselves a city, with a tower that reaches to the heavens, so that we may make a name for ourselves and not be scattered over the face of the whole earth." Genesis 11:4

With no spiritual guidance, man does what is right in his own sight. They were interested in serving themselves and not their Creator. Today, God is calling us back to oneness and has given us a spiritual common language so that He may do great exploits in the natural world through believers. God expects our spiritual unity and dependency to be like His with Jesus and the Holy Spirit.

"My prayer is not for them alone. I pray also for those who will believe in me through their message, that all of them may be one, Father, just as you are in me and I am in you. May they also be in us so that the world may believe that you have sent me. I have given them the glory that you

gave me, that they may be one as we are one—I in them and they in me—so that they may be brought to complete unity. Then the world will know that You sent me and have loved them even as You have loved me." John 17:20-23

THE EARLY CHURCH

In the book of Acts, we see a different type of market-force. It shows a church that was sharing and dependent on each other. Needs were being met that did not require the world system. The wrong message here is that God wanted them to spread the gospel not congregate in one place. Common sharing principles are not the problem, but they are the principles that can break the back of the world market system which was devised out of self-interest, selfishness, and greed.

"So, we urged Titus since he had earlier made a beginning, to bring also to completion this act of grace on your part. But just as you excel in everything—in faith, in speech, in knowledge, in complete earnestness and in your love for us see that you also **excel in this grace of giving***."* 2 Corinthians 8:6

"At the present time, your plenty will supply what they need, so that in turn their plenty will supply what you need. Then there will be equality," 2 Corinthians 8:14
"He who gathered much did not have too much, and he who gathered little did not have too little." Exodus 16:18 The Lion's Market turns capitalism 'on its head' prioritizing the principle of giving. The ROI (return on investment) that God promises is substantial, 'it will be given back to you pressed down and shaken together'.

"And they continued steadfastly in the apostles' doctrine and fellowship, in the breaking of bread, and in prayers. Then fear came upon every soul, and many wonders and signs were done through the apostles. Now all who believed were together, and had all things in common, and

sold their possessions and goods, and divided them among all, as anyone had need of. So continuing daily with one accord in the temple, and breaking bread from house to house, they ate their food with gladness and simplicity of heart, praising God and having favor with all the people. And the Lord added to the church daily those who were being saved." Acts 2:40-47

Barnabas sold his land and gave the proceeds to the church. This is the kind of generosity will break the back of the world system. Supply will come through the hands of saints.

"And Joses, who was also named Barnabas by the apostles (which is translated Son of Encouragement), a Levite of the country of Cyprus, having land, sold it, and brought the money and laid it at the apostles' feet. " Acts 4:36,37

A Prophet said a famine was coming and they gave gifts. *"Believe the Lord and you shall be established, believe **in the prophet** and you shall prosper."* 1 Chronicles 20:20

"And in these days prophets came from Jerusalem to Antioch. Then one of them, named Agabus, stood up and showed by the Spirit that there was going to be a great famine throughout all the world, which also happened in the days of Claudius Caesar. Then the disciples, each according to his ability, determined to send relief to the brethren dwelling in Judea. This they also did and sent it to the elders by the hands of Barnabas and Saul." Acts 11:27-30

As we look at these scriptures we see that unity and one heart is a key to Godly living and success in the Lion's Market. Divine order is bigger than you or me. The divine function is connection within the body. Connection to others and relationships will bring blessing to the world.

JACOB AND LABAN

The example of dependence/connection and alignment can be seen in the story of Laban and Jacob found in Genesis chapters 29 and 30. Jacobs's presence was a blessing for Laban in the 'Market Place' in which Laban was a participant (the world's). Laban became rich because of the promise on Jacob's life. Jacob came to Laban with nothing but worked hard and was blessed beyond measure and ultimately left with great wealth.

Through the process, Jacob's character was changed from sup- planter to a person who worked uprightly for a fair wage (and eventually Jacob would wrestle with God and earn the new name of 'Israel'). Jacob was a great example of living the principles of God even though his wages were changed seven times by Laban, he became prosperous.

Later at the end of the connection and break of unity Jacob was accused by Laban of stealing all the possessions but, God had revealed strategies on how to change the system in his favor.

Laban was not happy when he realized that Jacob had profited extensively while in his employ. After their final and very tense meeting, Laban came to the realization that Jacob had acted righteously and worked very hard while with him. In so doing he 'broke the back' of the world system and added tremendous assets to the growing lineage of Abraham.

In this last reformation, God is disclosing to men and women how to beat the world market in order to provide for His people in the coming days. Not to cheat but overcome through Godly wisdom. God is not about the short-term, but about the eternal.

THE WORLD'S RESPONSE

Coming against the greed and selfishness that is the foundation of the world system will bring a response. And not a favorable one! When the principles of the Lion's Market (giving, volunteerism, love, etc.) bring greater returns we can expect that some will want to connect (Yay!) but some will reject and demonize it. **Do not be surprised at some backlash from the world system.**

We see a good example of this in Acts chapters 6 and 7 where we find the account of Stephen one of the first group of deacons in the early church.

"Now in those days, when the number of the disciples was multiplying, there arose a complaint against the Hebrews by the Hellenists, because their widows were neglected in the daily distribution. Then the twelve summoned the multitude of the disciples and said, "It is not desirable that we should leave the word of God and serve tables. Therefore, brethren, seek out from among you seven men of good reputation, full of the Holy Spirit and wisdom, whom we may appoint over this business; but we will give ourselves continually to prayer and to the ministry of the word. And the saying pleased the whole multitude. And they chose Stephen, a man full of faith and the Holy Spirit, and Philip, Prochorus, Nicanor, Timon, Parmenas, and Nicolas, a proselyte from Antioch, whom they set before the apostles; and when they had prayed, they laid hands on them." Acts 6: 1-6

As this story unfolds, Stephan is performing his deacon duties delivering food to the needy all the while being full of faith and power, doing great wonders and signs. This was upsetting the order of things and upsetting the community's religious leaders. They tried to argue with Stephan, but the Lord gave him wisdom which they could not refute. So, they arranged for false witnesses to make accusations against him and you know how the story ends.

*"Then they secretly induced men to say, "We have heard him speak blasphemous words against Moses and God." And they stirred up the people, the elders, and the scribes; and they came upon him, seized him, and brought him to the council. They also set up false witnesses who said, "This man does not cease to speak blasphemous words against this holy place and the law; for we have heard him say that this Jesus of Nazareth will destroy this place and **change the customs** which Moses delivered to us."* Acts 6:11-14

One of their accusations was that the Christians were trying to 'Change their Customs', do things differently, change the system they had been in control of for generations. And this would affect not only their control of the people but also the wealth the made off of the people.

Mess with people's money/position/control and expect a FIGHT!

This is where our connections and relationships can really pay off. When we have produced a product that is more successful than the world-market we also have the fruit of solid relationships with the parties involved in the product. Those relationships can now be leveraged as the world-market retaliates. Anyone who has been in a fight understands the benefit of having an ally standing with them.

19
UNITY
Agreement is Powerful... and Required!

"Then I said to them, 'You see the trouble we are in: Jerusalem lies in ruins, and its gates have been burned with fire. Come, let us rebuild the wall of Jerusalem, and we will no longer be in disgrace.' I also told them about the gracious hand of my God on me and what the king had said to me. They replied, "Let us start rebuilding." So they began this good work." Nehemiah 2:17,18

"Without a vision, people will perish." Prov 29:18

Nehemiah knew that the vision he had to rebuild Jerusalem's wall and gates must take place within each family. The huge undertaking could not happen unless each family took responsibility for a small part. We see that each family did see it as a do-able assignment and that it was a work sanctioned by God.

In the Gospel of Matthew, it clearly reveals that unity is necessary so that our prayers are not hindered. This section also provides a process to reunite church members who have gotten out of alignment and need loving and sanctified correction and guidance. Later, we see (in Matthew 6:18) it also gives us the power to bind and loose.

UNITY WITH BOTH GOD AND MAN

Agreement allows us to connect to the Father and receive what we ask (which He has, in affect caused us to ask for in the first place). By uniting together, we bring God into our fellowship and this allows us to partner with God in manifesting His will on earth as it is in Heaven.

"*Moreover, if thy brother shall trespass against thee, go and tell him his fault between thee and him alone: if he shall hear thee, thou hast gained thy brother. But if he will not hear thee, then take with thee one or two more, that in the mouth of two or three witnesses every word may be established. And if he shall neglect to hear them, tell it unto the church: but if he neglects to hear the church, let him be unto thee as a heathen man and a publican. Verily I say unto you, Whatsoever ye shall bind on earth shall be bound in heaven: and whatsoever ye shall loose on earth shall be loosed in heaven.* **Again, I say unto you, that if two of you shall agree on earth as touching anything that they shall ask, it shall be done for them of my Father which is in heaven. For where two or three are gathered together in my name, there am I in the midst of them.**" Matthew 6:15-20

We see that with unity of purpose you can build a city even when the world is against it. If the leaders and people would have stopped at the first sign of adversity, Jerusalem would never have been rebuilt. On a whole, the task seemed too large but when each family took a gate and section of wall it was a small enough for them to have the vision to accomplish it. Nehemiah had the complete vision and passion for the work, but each family also had to have its own.

Today, God is calling for the Church to rise up and be a Kingdom builder. Jesus has set the goal: "Thy Kingdom come, and Thy will be done on earth that is in heaven". God wants his body to be fitly joined together. Each part creates a system to unveil His body on earth. Let this Church be the Church which will usher in the coming of Christ.

The New Jerusalem is coming to earth as seen in by the book of Revelation and God has destined us to take leadership roles as a unified body. The devil has successfully fragmented the body of believers into camps hindering our impact the world system. But God is saying 'No more!' We have to work together as in the book of Acts to bring unity back to the body of Christ.

As you notice in the book of Matthew when brothers stray from the truth we need to understand the importance of restoring relationships so that unity does not remain broken. God is saying that in our unity He will be in the midst of us that agree and in that agreement we will hear His will clearly and have confidence that what we ask of Him will be given. What a powerful word to connect, to agree and let Jesus be revealed to the world.

This connection and unity will allow the church to do projects that will change our cities states and nations. All that has been developed on the foundation of greed will be destroyed. Men and women will work to do what is right in God's sight. Remember, in unity that whatever we ask and agree on God will bring forth.

To affect the world system, we must demonstrate agreement and the love of unity to dwell in one mind and one accord. This is not a quick fix gospel message but an exhortation for each Christian to pursue a right mindset to be in unity and live for God and be unified in the body of Christ.

COVENANT HOUSE PROVISION

I was going through a difficult time when I had lost most everything. My life was turned upside down when my wife requested a divorce and left me for another man. I was devastated stuck with over 100,000 thousand dollars we had in debt. I had no place to go but back to the first home I'd ever purchased which we had been renting out but had not been for last few months. The previous renters had destroyed the property inside out and the mortgage was due.

My marriage had failed and there was no hope of restoration. I had no choice but to have God bring healing and restoration to my soul and life. All our property that had mortgages was given to me during the divorce. But what seemed to be a complete disaster turned to my favor when the Lord woke me up to a plan.

I had two properties that had little value. The Lord showed me that if I purchased a washed out 25 ft lot which was on the water it would turn my two lots into waterfront property. What had not been valuable before the divorce because of the mortgages now became valuable.

Sure enough, the purchase was by faith and with help from my best friend and the plan God gave me worked. The two now waterfront lots sold, and I paid off my debts. The best thing was God informed me to immediately write out my tithes and provide the gift to the Covenant House. With God's urgency, I traveled an hour and left the money which was nearly to the penny what they needed for an AC project. The ducting still needed to be done and they had no money to pay the vendor, but God knew how to put it all together.

I have always tried to live the best devoted life with integrity and God saw my heart and delivered me out of my woes. However, the best thing He had taken care of was others through my pain. My heart to give and be a volunteer through my faith is the Lion's Kingdom at work.
The Lion's Market works outside the church to bless people with God's compassion and grace. God loves and has compassion on all of mankind. A local hospital closed that had been built in the 50's. The reasons were bad management and an unmaintained facility

God put in my heart a desire to build another modern hospital and see if one of the near local hospitals would take over its management. If doctors are working out of surgical centers doing all major surgeries, why not a small 25 bed hospital with an excellent ER/Surgery center? What I found was that God united me with others with the same desire.

In the planning process, I needed to raise 25M dollars for the facility. I had no money, but God knew the hearts of people that would volunteer and cooperate. He knew the men and women who were in a position that could contribute and provide the dollars that were needed. God then started lining up corporations and organizations that would benefit from the new modern hospital. The local real estate, business, economic development and tourism was in desperate need of small, viable hospital. Both visitors and locals understood the need, but the question was how to solve the problem?

Creating a strong committee that believed in the mission was a necessity. Thus, God put a friend in my camp called Jim Mc Knight and we began our mission. Presenting the finding of a local community survey revealed not only the need but they were behind the idea. Once the idea came out and choosing the right medical organization, Sacred Heart, the key leaders moved forward.

We were able to start with $6M and 25 acres (with infrastructure) being donated! The State government, the Governor's Office and local government started projects that would guarantee a future home. The local government along with Sacred Heart agreed that our proposed 25 bed hospital would be viable however, we needed more funds. So, we came up with an idea for a half-cent sales tax to pay off the total debt. Jim and I agreed this could be achieved through a super-majority vote of the county commissioners.

What seemed impossible to the World Market mindset, raising taxes, became the guarantee for the future of the new hospital and some would say the community. One of proudest moments was when I asked for the vote that 4 out 4 commissioners voted for ½ cent sales tax. When voted on that night the people in the audience stood up and started clapping. Who would ever think people would clap for a tax?

Because of this action, a new hospital exists today in the community. What seemed impossible is possible when you are led in the mountain that God gives you. You must walk in integrity and truth and always remember that it's not about you. Lion's Market requires us to volunteer in our mountain of influence and boldly proceed in the favor that God lines up for us to take action. God promises that He will lead us, the problem is most people don't want to follow Him.

Lion's Market thinking comes down to you recognizing God within you wants to show His love and mercy to mankind. It is true, the Bible says, "when we were yet sinners, Christ died for us" (Romans 5:8). We forget that God so loved the world he gave his only begotten Son. This is the reason in my health care mountain that I know God cares.

After being appointed to my job, I had the great task to impact the health system of the community. With only three private doctors working in the community. they were a desperate need for health for all. We needed a place where regardless of the ability to pay or income level we must have quality health care. It is important to remember that we represent the King and we must do our best.

With the right attitude and actions, God will use your abilities to accomplish His will. Remember, as Bishop Hamon teaches, the Word the Will the Way. You never go against the Word of God and must line up with God's character that he reveals to us in the 66 books of the Bible. Second, we must hear the Rhema Word that is the 'now' word full of life, hope and love. This is the Will of God when he informs us through actions and thoughts what he wants us to do. It is the Call on our life and destiny of the vision he places in our heart.

For me it was me praying on how to solve the problem of access to health care in the community. It started with a new dental clinic that God let me create for the working poor. I changed how we do business and payer mix to make things solvent and sustainable.

After this business venture, I was reading Federal law and God opened my eyes to Community Health Centers, called FQHC's. What I thought seemed impossible He showed in the law exemptions to apply for grants. It was as if the text jumped out of the page in bold letters. God revealed the His will for a grant that would shift the health care system.

I begin to work on the idea and jump through all the hoops and applied for a large grant. You guessed it, we won the grant. The will of God acted, and God opened the door. From that grant the community received over time, a primary care center, mental health, dental, orthopedic, X-ray, and a women's center. Our facility was considered the best quality care in the area and we had 100% access regardless of the ability to pay. What seemed impossible required vision for a Lion's Market approach that results in Glory to God and life and hope for the community.

20

KINGDOM LABOR
The Work of God and Man

God

"*Thus the heavens and the earth, and all the host of them were finished. And on the seventh day, God ended His work which He had done, and He rested on the seventh day from all His work which He had done.*" Genesis 1:1,2

"*Six days you shall labor and do all your **work**, but the seventh day is the Sabbath of the LORD your God.*" Exodus 20:9

Man

"*The LORD God took the man and put him in the Garden of Eden to **work** it and take care of it. Heb 11 We see that faith without **works** is dead.*" Genesis 2:14-16 (New King James Version)

KINGDOM ARTISANS

"*Then the LORD spoke to Moses, saying: "See, I have called by name Bezalel the son of Uri, the son of Hur, of the tribe of Judah. And I have filled him with the Spirit of God, in wisdom, in understanding, in knowledge, and in all manner of workmanship, to design artistic works, to work in gold, in silver, in bronze, in cutting jewels for setting, in carving wood, and to work in all manner of workmanship. "And I, indeed I, have appointed with him Aholiab the son of Ahisamach, of the tribe of Dan; and I have put wisdom in the hearts of all the gifted artisans, that they may make all that I have commanded you: the tabernacle of meeting, the ark of the Testimony and the mercy seat that is on it, and all the furniture of the tabernacle." Exodus 31:1-7*

'Labor' or 'work' are not words, that damn or condemn someone but is a part of God's nature and character. God made man in His own image and man's nature requires work to be done. The question for each person is 'is my labor before the Lord?'

We were born to be workers and we will not feel accomplished unless we complete the very nature of God in us. God worked 6 days and it was good and he rested. We need to have the attitude to work and labor as unto God. The very nature of God was to labor and be creative and we as His children should take on the same responsibility for success.

As Christians we should take the same vision and attitude to be very best with the three A's Attitude, Ability, Action these characteristics should enhance our ability to get jobs and bless our organizations or partnerships in business. However, these days it seems we run from responsibility and we take the back seat in providing the answer to the world system. We need to take the attitude that we can change the world for the better because we can hear the voice of God.

We need to be a clear example in each one the seven mountain kingdoms and be a positive influence on policy and work ethics. I have seen several times people being poor examples as Christians by not following through our word. God demanded that vows to fulfilled and for our, Yes to Yes and No be No. Even though the children of Israel were misled by the Gibeonites they had to full fill their word. A Christian's word should be a sign of hope, surety, and truth. Gibeonites were not destroyed just because they proved to be crafty and the Israelites dull.

In Genesis chapter 31 we see that God can fill each person with His Spirit, in wisdom, in understanding, in knowledge, and in all *manner of* workmanship, design, and artistic works, to work and finish the best to the world to marvel over.

Even today we marvel over the music from Bach and the art from Michelangelo the artist. We marvel at the architecture, writings and all kinds of discoveries because of Christians.

They recognized that their gifts and talents originate from God. Our vision comes from a Godly life to include his spiritual guidance in the labor we do in this world. Not only sculpture but in government, management skills and moral policies that is unchangeable no matter which generation you are from.

INTEGRITY IS NOT AN OPTION

We see that today's world market which is based on greed and self-interest is wrong. Business leaders who are liars, robbers, thieves can run major business and steal millions because of their wrong leadership. Private business is no better than government when both basic foundations originate from a foundation of greed.

No longer do we have Statements in government and no longer do we see integrity prevail in private business. Each builds their foundation from quicksand in a belief that morals and values are variable in whatever arena you live. However, in the last financial crises of 2007, we see that this line of financial reasoning was wrong. While if we use the Bible as the author of truth it will bring enlightenment to problems and answer that will be Rhema word for government and private businesses.

The Bible teaches us true wisdom come from a Godly fear that he will be our judge then we take a different view on our actions. In the book of Revelation, it talks about knowledge increasing in the last days which has truly occurred with the computers and the information system. But it never says anything about Wisdom? It seems we stray from this word because we see it as a variable.

There is no concrete in wisdom or truth since we do not use the Holy Spirit to give us guidance. I'm not talking about dogma but being a rose in the desert, or fresh word in confusion. Many times, God has used me in my business to see through the confusion to the best answer in a board meeting. When this happens to me I see it as God allowing me to capture the right method, answer or process. You must have the heart of God and the people at heart in decisions. Decisions based on greed create protective nature of people and self-interest shines through. We need to be like Jacob and work for our blessing since it is God's nature.

WELFARE, GOD'S WAY

When God wanted to feed the poor, He made arrangement in several different ways. One that impresses me is the necessity to leave the fields after the first gleaning for the poor. The edges and the fields leftovers were left for the poor according to the law. This method of giving to the poor is found in the book of Ruth. Ruth gleaned the fields after the harvesters went through the grain so that he mother law and she could survive from Boaz's fields. *Ruth 2:3 Then she left and went and gleaned in the field after the reapers. And she happened to come to the part of the field belonging to Boaz, who was of the family of Elimelech. [7] And she said,*

'Please let me glean and gather after the reapers among the sheaves.' So she came and has continued from morning until now, though she rested a little in the house." And Boaz answered and said to her, "It has been fully reported to me,

all that you have done for your mother-in-law since the death of your husband, and how you have left your father and your mother and the land of your birth, and have come to a people whom you did not know before. The LORD repay your work, and a full reward be given you by the LORD God of Israel, under whose wings you have come for refuge."

The amazing story is the poor had to work for a living just as the field workers did. This is a great example of a different mindset to feed the poor. I believe it is the nature of man to work for a living as it is the nature of God to labor FIRST, and then rest. The poor in the Lion's Market should be given the 'second gleaning' in many business and agriculture settings.

Our waste could feed many if we follow this Biblical principle. No, we should not do unlimited handouts! We need to provide a way, so the poor do not have to wait for a government bailout but work in some way for their provisions. The poor can have self-respect and work for their provisions and have opportunity to learn to live with hope for their future.

21
KINGDOM WELFARE

'Welfare' is a word that has turned into something with an often- negative connotation here in the United States. We think of welfare recipients as those who are in poverty due to laziness.
200 years ago, though, it meant the well-being of an individual or population relating to safety, health and, happiness.

Even the US constitution uses the word 'welfare' in the preamble:
"*We the People of the United States, in Order to form a more perfect Union, establish Justice, insure domestic Tranquility, provide for the common defense, promote the general Welfare, and secure the Blessings of Liberty to ourselves and our Posterity, do ordain and establish this Constitution for the United States of America.*"

This understanding of the word has nothing to do with public assistance. The US Constitution I believe, is trying to set up a systemic means of protection that positions an individual's whole state of welfare to improve their lives. Our government is simply supposed to be providing the opportunity to allow all citizens to live healthy, safe and happy lives.

In God's Kingdom, looking after our welfare is something the King does! Hallelujah, the King is for us as His subjects, as His children and co-heirs with His Son Jesus Christ.
He says through the Apostle John in 3 John 2 (NKJV)
"Beloved, I pray that you may prosper in all things and be in health, just as your soul prospers."

OUR APPETITES

The determining factor is the appetite of the soul. The soul shows the characteristics of the man; hunger, joy, peace, sadness, bitterness, love etc. We can choose to starve it or fill it with proper experiences. It is not the mind's knowledge but how we exist in our nature, our being.

The soul with proper (Godly) prosperity will have great welfare. The soul is part of our being that will live forever, either in heaven or hell. Since Jesus died for all souls, it's **our choice** to choose which place we spend forever in (our eternal welfare). We received what God had planned since before the Garden of Eden, eternal life. Now it is our choice as freewill moral agents (Tree of Knowledge) to choose the state of our welfare now and forever.

Our soul and spirit are everlasting, what God wants is our soul, which is our appetites and desires, to choose to find satisfaction and purpose in His ways. If our soul prospers it will affect external prosperity as well as health AND that of those around us. Kingdom welfare is the prosperity of the soul. Hungering and thirsting after righteousness means our soul's appetite is for God. We stop what we are doing motivated by our 'flesh' and eat of the Lord's table to satisfy the hunger signals.

HUNGER AND THIRST FOR RIGHTEOUSNESS

We must actively choose God, it is not a passive activity, or we will die from starvation. Eat the Word as our meat, it is our Manna from Heaven and drink the Word as our water that is life- giving and that flows from beneath His throne. Are we going to try to fill our appetites with other foods the corrupt things of this world? The children of Israel had started to miss the food they had in Egypt while they wandered in the wilderness. So, they cried out for meat in an attempt to satisfy their hunger. God sent them an abundance of quail and you remember how that turned out right? (see Numbers chapter 11 if you don't know).

Look at this sobering (if not scathing) passage from the book of James:

"Where do wars and fights come from among you? Do they not come from your desires (appetites) for pleasure that war in your members? You lust and do not have. You murder and covet and cannot obtain. You fight and war. Yet you do not have because you do not ask. You ask and do not receive, because you ask amiss, that you may spend it on your pleasures. Adulterers and adulteresses! Do you not know that friendship with the world (hunger for worldly things) is enmity with God? Whoever therefore wants to be a friend of the world makes himself an enemy of God." ***James 4:1-5***

"If you seek the Lord with your heart and soul you will find Him." Matthew 16:26

"For what is a man profited, if he shall gain the whole world, and lose his own soul? or what shall a man give in exchange for his soul?" Deuteronomy 4:28

Our welfare has been 'bought with a price', so choose life! Silver and gold are not the backbone of the Lion's Market welfare program, miracles of healing will be the children's bread.

"Then Peter said, 'Silver and gold I do not have, but what I do have I give you: In the name of Jesus Christ of Nazareth, rise up and walk'." Act 3:6

Jesus' message of not meat and drink, but love, joy and peace to all who may come brings true welfare in the Kingdom of God.

"For the [pagan] Gentiles eagerly seek all these things; [but do not worry,] for your heavenly Father knows that you need them. But first and most importantly seek (aim at, strive after) His kingdom and His righteousness [His way of doing and being right—the attitude and character of God], and all these things will be given to you also. So, do not worry about tomorrow; for tomorrow will worry about itself. Each day has enough trouble of its own."
Matthew 6:32-34 (AMP)

Hallelujah! God is in control of our welfare!

22

MAMMON
The Conclusion

To counter and subjugate the World Market we need to recognize the divine disrupters that bring supernatural abundance along with confusion to mankind's mammon-based economic system.

First is Giving. It breaks the logic of wants, needs and greed that drives people. Second is Volunteerism which destroys selfishness and wants plus the concept that it is all about me. Third, Stewardship which brings an end to paralysis and creates the army of action. Christians who fail to serve others were judged by Jesus. He said if you want to be my disciple then you must serve one another. Finally, is the destruction of the love of money which destroys the god called mammon.

Working using God's principals allows for a reward at the end of our life. Show me your works motivated by faith and I will show you the remnants of your faith walk, your true legacy.

"No one can serve two masters. Either you will hate the one and love the other; or else you will be devoted to one and despise the other. **You cannot serve both God and Mammon.***"* Matthew 6:24

Mammon is the lust after material wealth, riches, and whose devotion to the accumulation wealth, with the greedy pursuit of gain. This demonic drive impacts our soulish appetite for a wealth-driven life that is the opposite of what

God wants. Loving your neighbor as yourself destroys the world economic system and its classes of haves and have-nots.

THE DECEPTION OF MAMMON

In the book of Acts chapter 1, we see the sharing of goods not for wealth but for the meeting of needs in the church community. But it was not long before the spirit of mammon tried to infiltrate the early church. In Acts chapter 5 we are given the account of a simple real estate deal that became deceptive and a husband and wife made a secret agreement which resulted in their deaths.

Why? The property and money were already theirs, but they had an ungodly desire for honor and prestige, so the couple manufactured a lie. A lie that was not against man but the Holy Spirit.

Today many sales and marketplace deals are filled with lies and uncovered by God. This mammon spirit demonstrates the greed of embezzlement that shows up regularly in the world market as we recently saw in the 2008 economic disaster. We as Christians must guard ourselves especially in missionary work and ministries from the spirit of mammon. I'm ashamed as a Christian every time I hear of a new report that a 'Christian' leader has been caught embezzling.

FAVOR OF THE LION'S MARKET

In the Book of Nehemiah, God does not pick leaders by men's standards but by their compassion and love for His people. At that time Jerusalem was filled with many Jews but fear and circumstance held them down with no hope. God was looking for a man after His own heart that would carry out a vision through a mission. Who He calls is He who qualifies.

Nehemiah was a wine taster by trade but to God, he was a facilitator. Not seeing his circumstance, he recognized his position. As he stepped out **IN FAITH** and announced his plan, the Babylonian King, leaders, and people volunteered to help with his call, God's Favor! The heathen king gave money, resources and time for God's plan to work. A foreign leader who was wicked in many respects followed the leading of a man who demonstrated integrity and truth.

Favor is for you in Lion's Market and for those secular men and women who are called to break the back of the enemy. You will be challenged like Nehemiah with accusations, mocking, laughter, threats of death, financial shortfalls and finally rebellion and accusations but none of it will stick because you have a decree and declaration from the King of all Kings.

We clearly see God's Economy and His Currency of Faith in Nehemiah's work and vision. The Lord used him to bring peace, restoration and prosperity to the oppressed population and rebooted the economy of the city of Jerusalem.

Now is the time for Christian business people, entrepreneurs, and leaders of all types to repent and shift up to the principles of the Lion's Market.

I firmly believe that together with the Lord and with each other we can shake the world economy in this final reformation!

God Bless You!

www.ingramcontent.com/pod-product-compliance
Lightning Source LLC
LaVergne TN
LVHW021408080426
835508LV00020B/2499